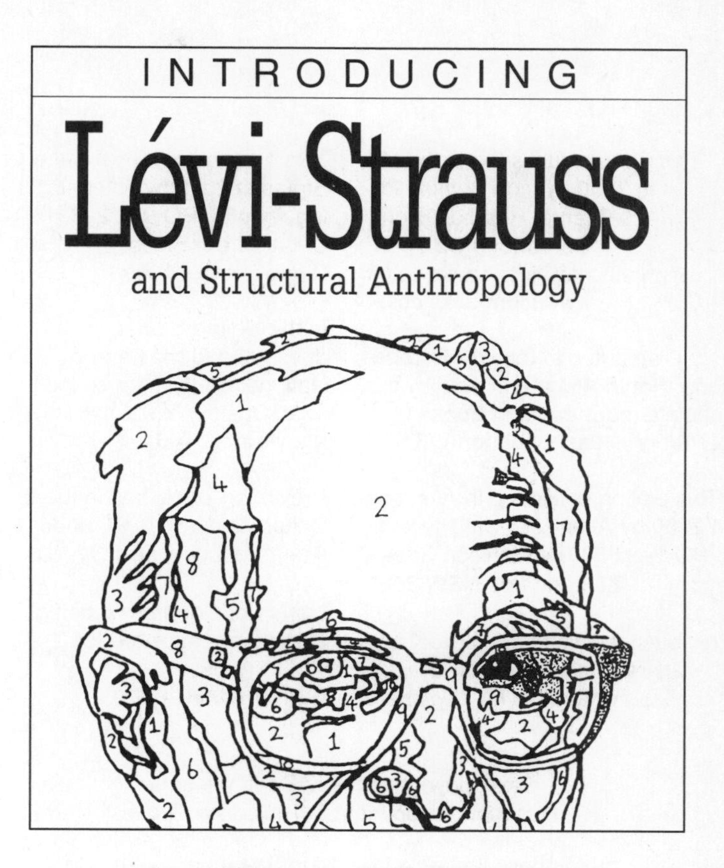

INTRODUCING Lévi-Strauss and Structural Anthropology

Boris Wiseman and Judy Groves

Edited by Richard Appignanesi

ICON BOOKS UK TOTEM BOOKS USA

This edition published in the UK
in 2000 by Icon Books Ltd.,
Grange Road, Duxford,
Cambridge CB2 4QF
email: info@iconbooks.co.uk
www.iconbooks.co.uk

Distributed in the UK, Europe,
Canada, South Africa and Asia by the
Penguin Group: Penguin Books Ltd.,
27 Wrights Lane, London W8 5TZ

This edition published in Australia
in 2000 by Allen & Unwin Pty. Ltd.,
PO Box 8500, 9 Atchison Street,
St. Leonards NSW 2065

Previously published in the UK and
Australia in 1997 under the title
Lévi-Strauss for Beginners

This edition published in the United
States in 2000 by Totem Books
Inquiries to: PO Box 223,
Canal Street Station,
New York, NY 10013

In the United States,
distributed to the trade by
National Book Network Inc.,
4720 Boston Way, Lanham,
Maryland 20706

Previously published in the
United States in 1998 under the
title *Introducing Lévi-Strauss*

Library of Congress catalog
card number applied for

ISBN 1 84046 147 0

Originating editor: Richard Appignanesi

Printed and bound in Australia
by McPherson's Printing Group, Victoria

A MEETING WITH LÉVI-STRAUSS

Claude Lévi-Strauss is one of the most influential thinkers of our time. One of his many achievements has been to place anthropology at the heart of the evolution of contemporary French thought. He set about systematically putting into place, from the ground up, entire new systems for explaining humanity to itself. In effect, he reinvented modern anthropology.

Since I was a child, I have been bothered by, let's call it the irrational, and have been trying to find an order behind what presents itself to us as a disorder.

During the 1950s and 60s, Lévi-Strauss's name became associated with a movement known as **structuralism** which was to influence the entire spectrum of disciplines that makes up the human sciences.

On a snowy afternoon, 19 November 1996, the author of this book interviewed Claude Lévi-Strauss at the Collège de France in Paris.

YOU HAVE REVEALED THE EXISTENCE OF A TIMELESS **PENSÉE SAUVAGE**, A "WILD" MODE OF THOUGHT, AT WORK AT THE HEART OF HUMAN SOCIETY.
I have tried to show that there is not a great difference between the ways of thinking of those cultures we call "primitive" and our own.

When, in our own societies, we notice customs or beliefs that appear strange or that contradict common sense, we explain them as the vestiges or the relics of archaic modes of thought. On the contrary, it seems to me that these modes of thought are still present and alive among us. We often give them free rein of expression, so that they have come to co-exist with other, domesticated, forms of thinking, such as those that come under the heading of science.

Lévi-Strauss has elaborated new theories in nearly all the key domains of anthropology. In doing so, he has also put into place a general theory of culture which emphasizes the importance of hidden structures, analogous to a kind of syntax, operating behind the scenes.

The origins of Lévi-Strauss's thought lie ultimately in the rainswept forests of the South American continent, home to the Caduveo, the Bororo and the Nambikwara. It was there that his encounter with "primitive" man first took place.

Claude Lévi-Strauss was born in Brussels in 1908. He was brought up in Paris's 16th *arrondissement* (where he still lives today) in a street named after the artist **Nicolas Poussin** (1594–1665), whom he came to admire and write about. His father was a portrait painter and his great-grandfather on his father's side, Isaac Strauss (born in Strasbourg in 1808), was a violinist, composer and conductor who worked with Berlioz and Offenbach.

Square
Rue Poussin
Donizetti
Place
Jean
The atmosphere in which I grew up was an artistic one. . . In my childhood, the 16th arrondissement was a more bohemian place than it is now. I recollect a farm at the end of our street.

In 1914, when the Great War broke out and his father was conscripted, Lévi-Strauss went to live with his mother and her sisters in the house of his maternal grandfather, the chief rabbi of Versailles.

MAURICE MERLEAU-PONTY

SIMONE DE BEAUVOIR

He studied law, then sat the *agrégation* in philosophy, which he taught in a secondary school (a subject still taught in French secondary schools today) until 1935.

I began reading Marx for the first time at the age of 17.

Among those preparing for the *agrégation* at the same time as Lévi-Strauss were **Maurice Merleau-Ponty** (1908–61) and **Simone de Beauvoir** (1908–86). French philosophy at the time was marked by its neo-Kantianism, and many traces of the thought of the great Enlightenment philosopher **Immanuel Kant** (1724–1804) can be found in Lévi-Strauss's work.

In 1935, disillusioned with philosophy, Lévi-Strauss accepted an offer to become a lecturer in sociology at the University of São Paulo in Brazil.

At the end of that academic year, I carried out, together with my wife, my first ethnographic expedition in the Matto Grosso region of Brazil.

This was his first encounter with the Bororo and the Caduveo whose unique mode of artistic expression – a complex form of body painting – he later analyzed in great detail.

"I thought I was re-living the adventures of the first explorers of the 16th century. I was once again discovering, but with my own eyes, the New World. Everything seemed fantastic to me: the landscapes, the animals, the plants." [CL-S]

It was during a later expedition in 1938 that Lévi-Strauss carried out field research among the Nambikwara, a semi-nomadic group with whom he lived for several months.

They were so destitute that a family's entire possessions could be contained in a single basket carried on a woman's back. They went about naked and slept on the bare ground.

Lévi-Strauss had discovered the "noble savages" celebrated by **Jean-Jacques Rousseau** (1712–78) and other 18th century Enlightenment philosophers.

After these two trips, however, Lévi-Strauss was soon to discover that he was more suited for the work of the cabinet anthropologist (ethnology) than for field work (ethnography).

But I was soon to return to America, this time for a different reason– the Second World War and the Nazi threat!

STRUCTURALISM
Anthropology and Psychoanalysis
A
B

It was in the New York public library in 1943 that Lévi-Strauss, then a Jewish refugee who had fled the German invasion of France, began work on what became his doctoral thesis and first book: *The Elementary Structures of Kinship*. This work revolutionized the anthropological study of kinship systems and established his reputation among professional anthropologists.

It was also at this time that Lévi-Strauss began to discover primitive art – not in ethnographic museums, but in the windows of New York antique dealers.
Primitive art was then considered by most anthropologists to have primarily a documentary value, but for me it represented more than that.
ANDRÉ BRETON

On the boat that took him to New York, Lévi-Strauss had encountered **André Breton** (1896–1966), the leader of the French Surrealist movement.

In New York, Breton introduced Lévi-Strauss to the German Surrealist artist **Max Ernst** (1891–1976), with whom he was to have a lasting friendship, and the art critic **George Duthuit** (1891–1973). The four men shared the same keen interest in primitive art, in particular Indian art.

WE SET OUT TO FIND NEW OBJECTS TO COLLECT.
WE POOLED OUR RESOURCES WHEN ONE OR OTHER OF US WAS UNABLE TO AFFORD A NEW ITEM.
MAX ERNST
GEORGE DUTHUIT

Many paths crossed at that time in New York. Other encounters with the Surrealists were at the origin of the American artistic movement that became known in the late 1940s as Abstract Expressionism.

In New York I had an important encounter with ROMAN JAKOBSON (1896-1982), the Prague School linguist.

I INTRODUCED LÉVI-STRAUSS TO THE AREA OF STRUCTURAL LINGUISTICS.

Within this linguistic discipline, Lévi-Strauss discovered the principles, methods and ideas that were to enable him to crystallize his own conceptions and develop what he was to call **structural anthropology**.

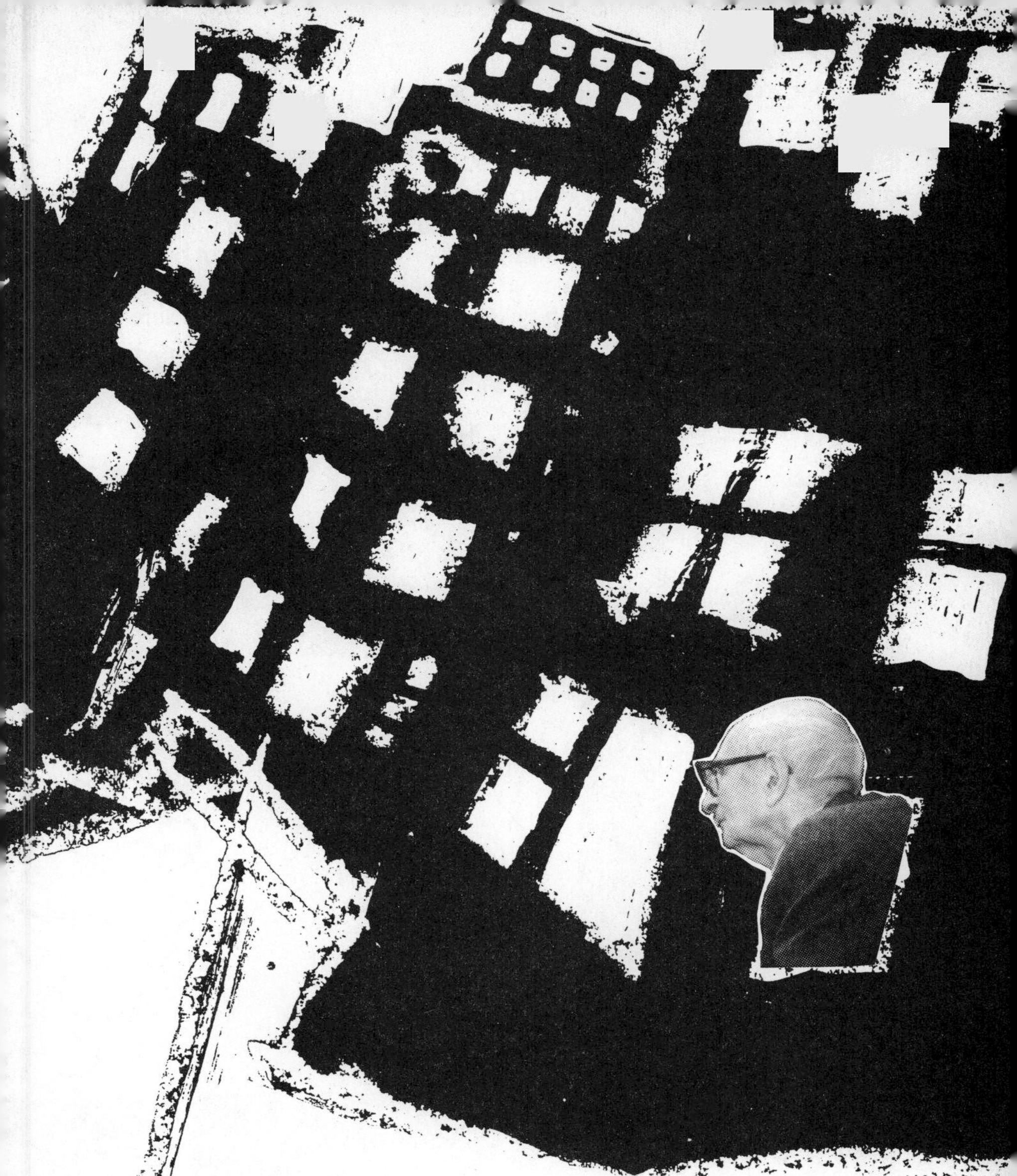

"New York – and this was the secret of its charm and fascination – was a town where everything seemed possible. Its social and cultural fabric, like the spreading town itself, was riddled with holes. One needed only to choose one, slip into it, and, like Alice on the other side of the looking glass, find oneself in a world so full of enchantments that it seemed unreal." [CL-S]

PIONEERS OF ANTHROPOLOGY: MALINOWSKI

In 1922, twenty-three years before Lévi-Strauss began his work on kinship systems, **Bronislaw Malinowski** (1884–1942), the great pioneer of field anthropology, published one of the best-known ethnographic treatises: *Argonauts of the Western Pacific.* It was the result of two extensive field trips carried out among the inhabitants of the Trobriand islands, an archipelago lying off the Southeastern end of New Guinea.

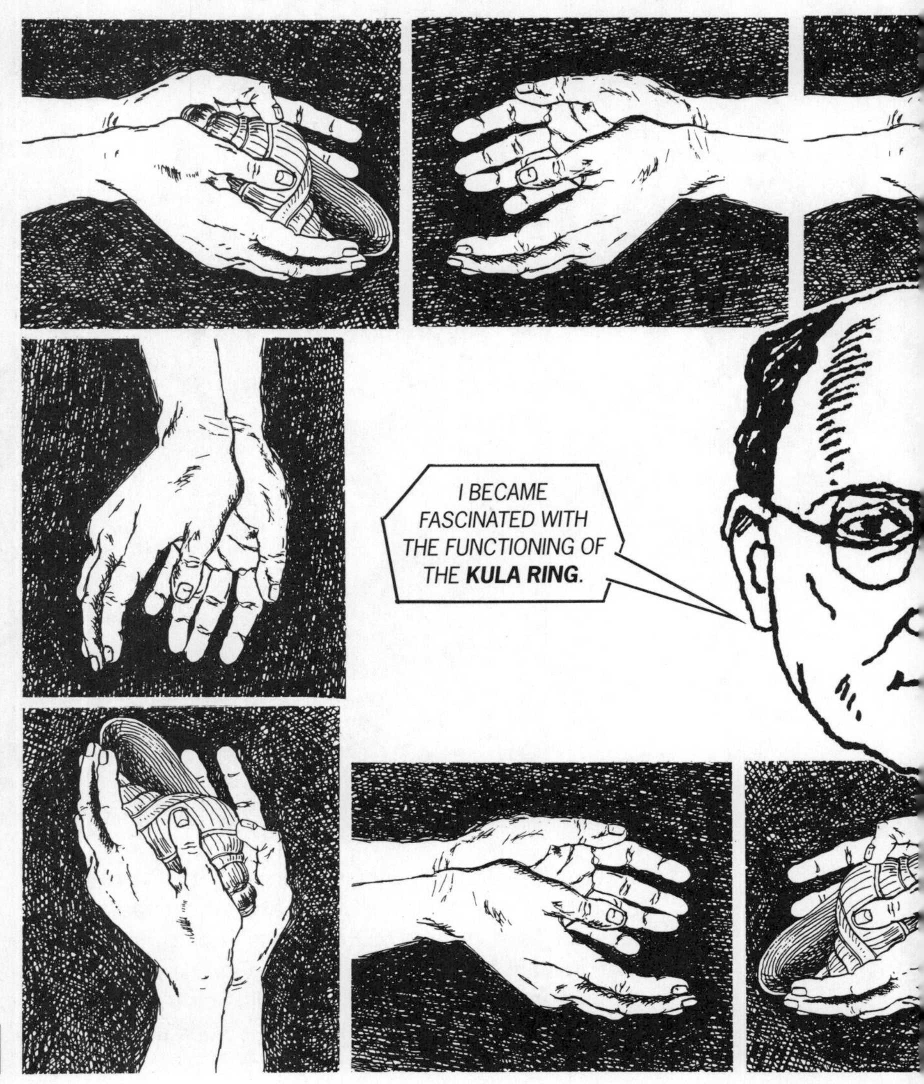
I BECAME FASCINATED WITH THE FUNCTIONING OF THE **KULA RING**.

The *kula ring* is a system of ceremonial gift exchanges, nearly 100 miles across, that links the numerous islands of the archipelago – a kind of early Internet! Malinowski described how, in this carefully regulated system of reciprocity, different types of ornaments (shell necklaces called *Soulava* and white arm bracelets called *Mwali*) travelled around the islands in different directions.

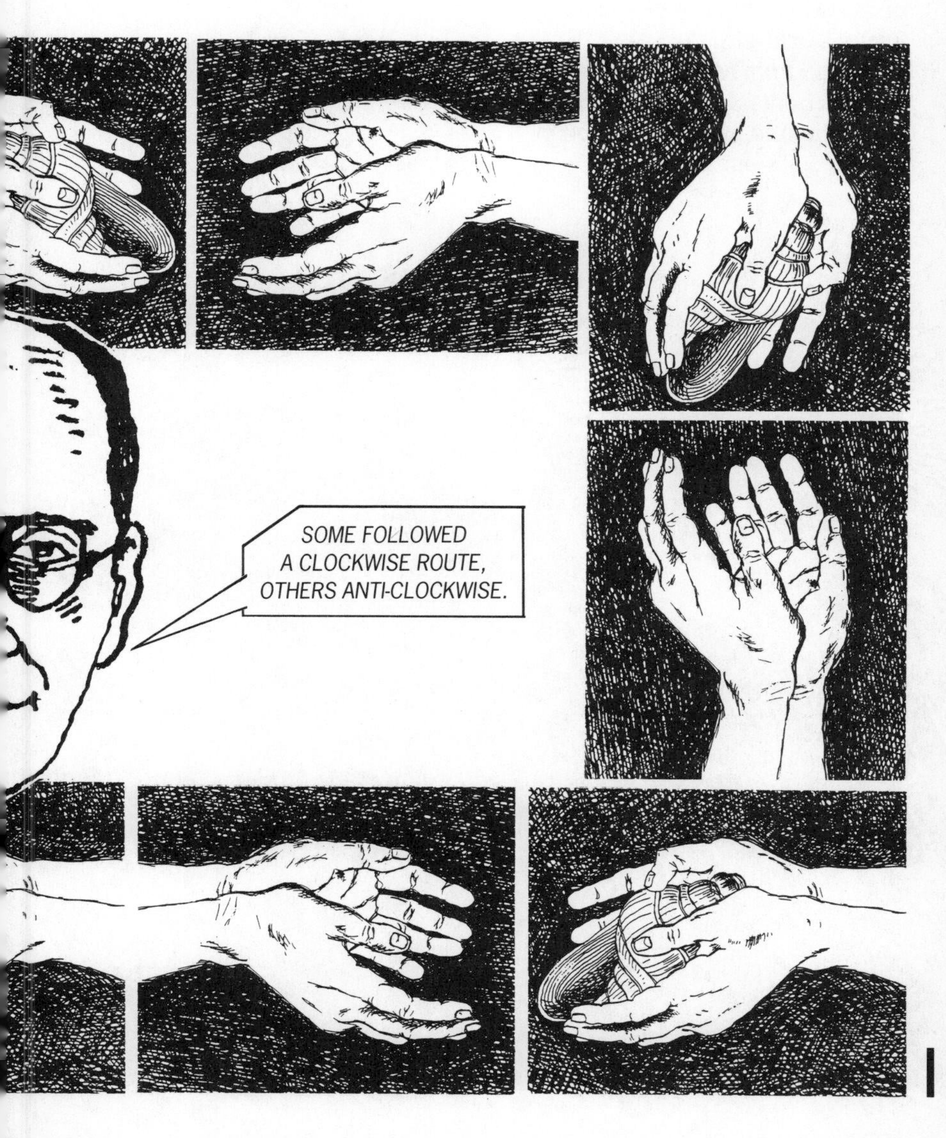
SOME FOLLOWED A CLOCKWISE ROUTE, OTHERS ANTI-CLOCKWISE.

MAUSS AND THE RULE OF RECIPROCITY

In his influential essay *The Gift* (1925), the great French sociologist **Marcel Mauss** (1872–1950) – nephew of a founder of sociology, **Emile Durkheim** (1859–1917) – extracted from Malinowski's vivid field accounts a general theory about the role of gift exchange in human cultures.

*I UNCOVERED IN PARTICULAR THE RULE OF **RECIPROCITY** GOVERNING SUCH EXCHANGES, WITH ITS BINDING TRIPLE OBLIGATION: TO GIVE, TO RECEIVE AND TO RETURN.*

Through Mauss's essay, Lévi-Strauss found the key to a new understanding of what kinship systems are and how they work. He proposed that marital alliances between groups took the classic form of a gift-exchange relationship and that the most important gifts exchanged were women. He thus came to see the function of kinship systems as regulating (and ensuring the continuity of) the exchange of women between groups.

It is exchange, always exchange, that emerges as the fundamental and common basis of all modalities of the institution of marriage.

WHY IS IT WOMEN WHO ARE EXCHANGED AND NOT MEN?
One argument is this: while men see the women who belong to their group as potential sexual partners, they recognize that these same women are also desired by men from other groups and are therefore a means of securing alliances with them.
DO WOMEN'S SEXUAL DESIRES NOT COME INTO THE PICTURE?
ACCORDING TO LÉVI-STRAUSS, NOT MUCH.

Lévi-Strauss also argues that if it is around women and not men that the system of reciprocity is organized, this is because it is through women that the biological continuity of the social group is ensured.

IN THIS RESPECT, WOMEN ARE THE GROUP'S MOST VALUABLE ASSETS.

In practice, how do such exchanges work? Lévi-Strauss offers a new solution to an old anthropological problem, that of **cross-cousin marriages**.

CROSS-COUSIN MARRIAGES

Anthropologists distinguish between parallel cousins, which are children of same-sex siblings (my father's brother's child or my mother's sister's child) and cross-cousins who are the children of siblings of different sexes (my mother's brother's child).

While it is often the case in primitive societies that the union of parallel cousins is considered to be incestuous and their marriage prohibited, marriage between cross-cousins is favoured and even prescribed.

BOTH RELATIONS ARE EQUALLY CLOSE (FIRST COUSINS), SO WHY IS ONE KIND OF UNION CONSIDERED INCESTUOUS AND PROHIBITED AND THE OTHER NOT?

Lévi-Strauss reduces the great variety of known kinship systems to a small number of elementary structures which he shows to involve one of two basic forms of exchange. These he labels "restricted" and "generalized". The first type consists basically of a straight swap between two groups and depends on a form of dualistic organization, such as the two-part division of a tribe into moieties.

In "generalized" exchange (marriage "in a circle"), the schema involves at least three groups related,

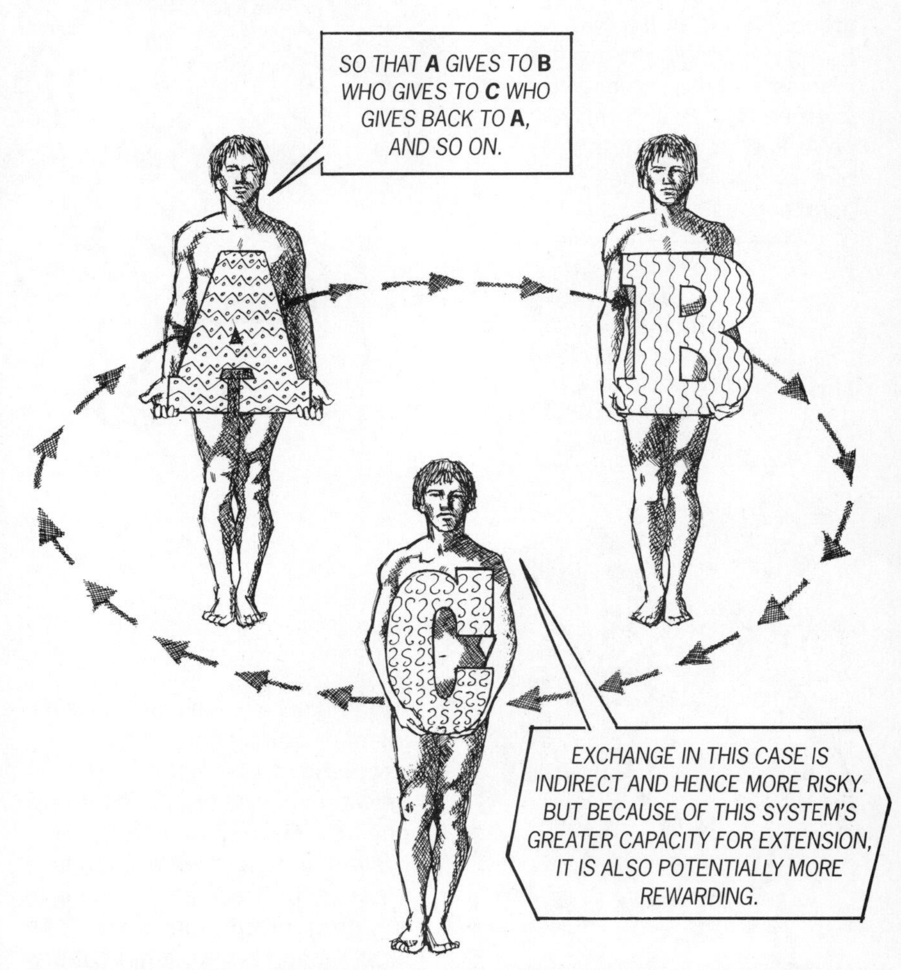
SO THAT **A** GIVES TO **B** WHO GIVES TO **C** WHO GIVES BACK TO **A**, AND SO ON.
A
B
C
EXCHANGE IN THIS CASE IS INDIRECT AND HENCE MORE RISKY. BUT BECAUSE OF THIS SYSTEM'S GREATER CAPACITY FOR EXTENSION, IT IS ALSO POTENTIALLY MORE REWARDING.

Cross-cousin marriage constitutes an **exemplary** instance of marriage by exchange since it also applies to societies that practice the "straight swap" system.

EXOGAMOUS AND ENDOGAMOUS MARRIAGES

The mechanics of this exchange system take some working out (thinking about kinship problems is always a bit of a brain teaser). Here is a simple hypothetical situation chosen from a patrilineal society – i.e. one in which membership of a group, such as a clan or moiety, is traced through the male line of descent.

Let's imagine two patrilineal groups, **A** and **B**. If a man (Kunga) belonging to group **A** marries a woman belonging to group **B**, their children will be **A**, and so will Kunga's brother's children, their parallel cousins.

BUT MY SISTER, WHO IS ALSO **A**, AND WHO MARRIES A MAN FROM **B**, WILL GIVE BIRTH TO CHILDREN WHO WILL BELONG TO GROUP **B**. THESE ARE MY CHILDREN'S CROSS-COUSINS.
A
B

B
A

A marriage between cross-cousins therefore corresponds to an **exogamous** marriage: a union between an individual from **A** and one from **B** which maintains the system of "restricted" exchange. Marriage between parallel cousins is **endogamous**: it involves all **A**s or all **B**s and is therefore contrary to the rule of exchange. It is prohibited because no social benefit is derived from it.

The above situation may be represented as follows:

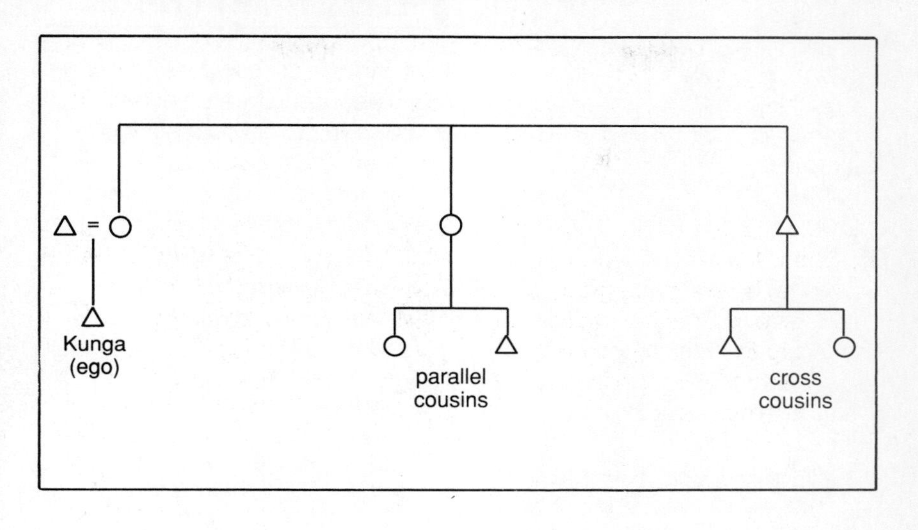
Kunga
(ego)
parallel
cousins
cross
cousins

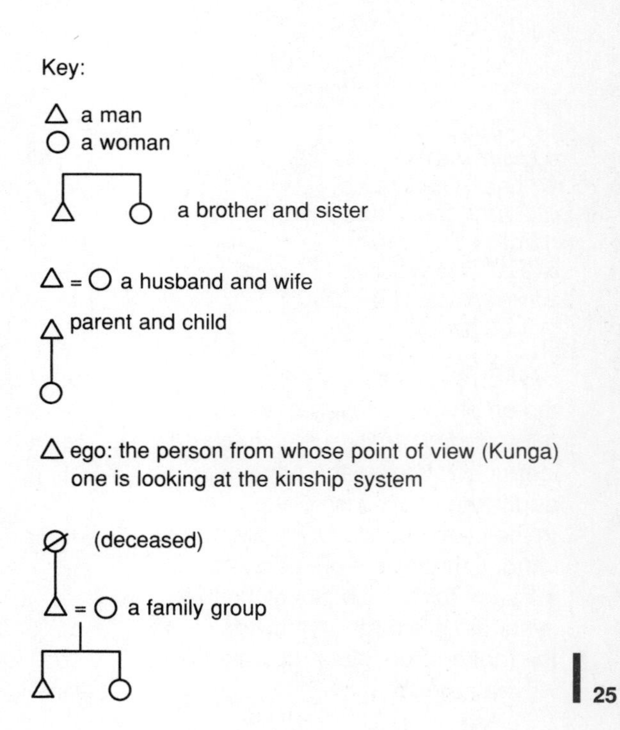
Key:
a man
a woman
a brother and sister
a husband and wife
parent and child
ego: the person from whose point of view (Kunga)
one is looking at the kinship system
(deceased)
a family group

WHAT IS THE "ELEMENTARY UNIT"?

Lévi-Strauss's kinship theory still gives rise to heated debate. It stands in radical opposition to other dominant theories, such as that developed by another great anthropologist, this time in the British tradition, **Sir Alfred Radcliffe-Brown** (1881–1955), in his *The Study of Kinship Systems* (1941).

THE UNIT OF STRUCTURE FROM WHICH KINSHIP IS BUILT UP IS THE GROUP WHICH I CALL AN "ELEMENTARY FAMILY", CONSISTING OF A MAN AND HIS WIFE AND THEIR CHILD OR CHILDREN.

What are elementary are not the families, which are isolated units, but the RELATIONSHIP between those units.

Lévi-Strauss's theory shifts the emphasis away from the "elementary family" which is no longer considered the point of departure of all kinship systems. In the Lévi-Straussian model, the various modalities of marital **alliance** form the basis of kinship systems. It is through marriage that the fabric of kinship structures is woven together.

THE SAUSSURIAN MODEL

Lévi-Strauss took up and applied to kinship one of the major themes of Saussurian linguistics.

*WHAT MATTERS IN LANGUAGE ARE NOT THE SOUND UNITS (PHONEMES) IN THEMSELVES, BUT THE **RELATIONSHIPS** BETWEEN SOUNDS.*

Ferdinand de Saussure (1857–1913), the inventor of structural linguistics, revolutionized the study of language by showing that the identity of each individual sound was defined **negatively** in relation to what it was not.

The word ***bat***, for example, is made up of three sounds or phonemes /**b**/ /**a**/ /**t**/, each of which fulfils a function in as much as it differs from the phonemes in other words such as ***mat***, ***bit*** and ***ban***.

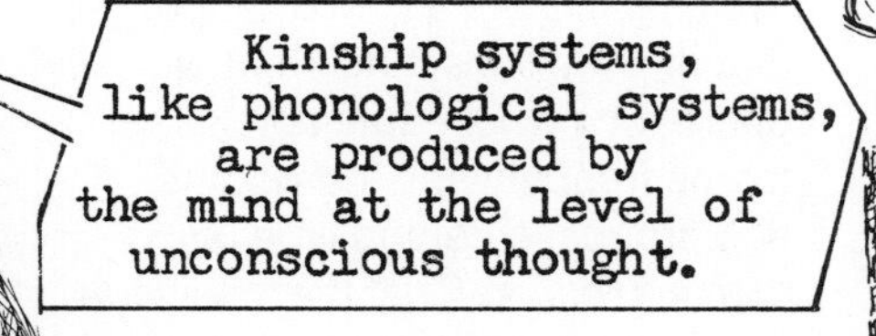
Kinship systems, like phonological systems, are produced by the mind at the level of unconscious thought.

KINSHIP IS COMMUNICATION

Underlying the whole of Lévi-Strauss's **alliance** theory is a fundamental analogy between kinship systems and language. This analogy takes different forms.

"The rules of marriage and kinship systems are like a kind of language, that is, they constitute a set of operations whose function is to ensure, between individuals and groups, a certain type of communication. That the 'message' consists here of *women* circulating between clans, lineages or families (and not, as in language itself, of *words* circulating between individuals) does not alter the fact that in both cases it is the same type of phenomenon that is being observed."

Lévi-Strauss here is playing on the different meanings of the word *communication*, giving it a more concrete, spatial sense which brings out the idea of circulating objects. One may recall here the *kula ring* which presents the image of a system of "communication" in this very way.

In terms of human evolution, I attribute to the emergence of language ("symbolic thought") a key role in setting into motion the entire system of reciprocity whereby women first came to be exchanged.

More, he argues that it is the emergence of language which predicates all other forms of exchange. This goes to the very core of Lévi-Strauss's early theory of culture. The basis upon which society and culture are constructed consists of circuits of exchange – exchanges of signs (words), of women, of goods and services. And it is the first of these circuits – the system of linguistic communication – that constitutes the foundations upon which the others rest.

THE INCEST TABOO

Throughout his writings on kinship there is a central enigma that Lévi-Strauss constantly returns to – that of the **incest taboo**. More precisely, he asks himself: why is it present, in one form or another, in all known human societies?

I rejected previous explanations of the taboo.

GENETIC ARGUMENTS THAT INVOKE THE RISK OF DEGENERACY.
PSYCHO-CULTURAL ARGUMENTS THAT INVOKE AN INSTINCTIVE HORROR, A DEFENCE AGAINST AN UNCONSCIOUS WISH.
OR, ON THE CONTRARY, AN INCAPACITY TO FEEL SEXUAL AROUSAL DUE TO THE PROXIMITY OF KIN.

Genealogical arguments, which see in the taboo the remnants of archaic institutions that have now disappeared, are also criticized. Durkheim and Freud provide two examples.
I RELATE THE INCEST TABOO TO RELIGIOUS PROHIBITIONS CONCERNING MENSTRUAL BLOOD, THEMSELVES SYMBOLICALLY LINKED TO THE BLOOD OF THE CLAN AND HENCE THE TOTEM.
DURKHEIM
AT THE DAWN OF HUMAN CULTURE, REBELLIOUS SONS KILLED AND ATE THEIR FATHER, AND THEN, FEELING REMORSE FOR THEIR DEED, SET UP THE FIRST PROHIBITIONS, FORBIDDING THEMSELVES THOSE VERY WOMEN THEY HAD DESIRED.
The theory of **Sigmund Freud** (1856–1939) in *Totem and Taboo* (1913) is relegated to the rank of "myth-making".
FREUD

THE RULE OF INCEST

So where does Lévi-Strauss depart from these previous theories?

Within the context of the theory of kinship that he develops around the principle of exchange, Lévi-Strauss relates the incest taboo to rules of exogamy that require marriage outside of a particular group or category of individuals. In short, the primary function of the incest taboo is to oblige individuals to marry out.

The prohibition of incest is less a rule prohibiting marriage with the mother, sister or daughter, than a rule obliging the mother, sister or daughter to be given to others. It is the rule of the gift PAR EXCELLENCE.

Thus, Lévi-Strauss solves the question of the universality of the incest taboo by revealing the sociological imperative – exchange – that makes its existence necessary.

And he proposes that it was together with, and *through,* the emergence of the rule of exogamy (enforced by incest restrictions) that the passage from a state of nature to a state of culture occurred.

The incest taboo is the first rule.

The introduction of an incest rule marks the replacement of arbitrary primate mating-patterns with regulated exchange. The incest taboo forces the kin group to make alliances with strangers, thereby creating a community based on ties that are other than those dictated by nature.

And it is these ties which constitute the context of culture.

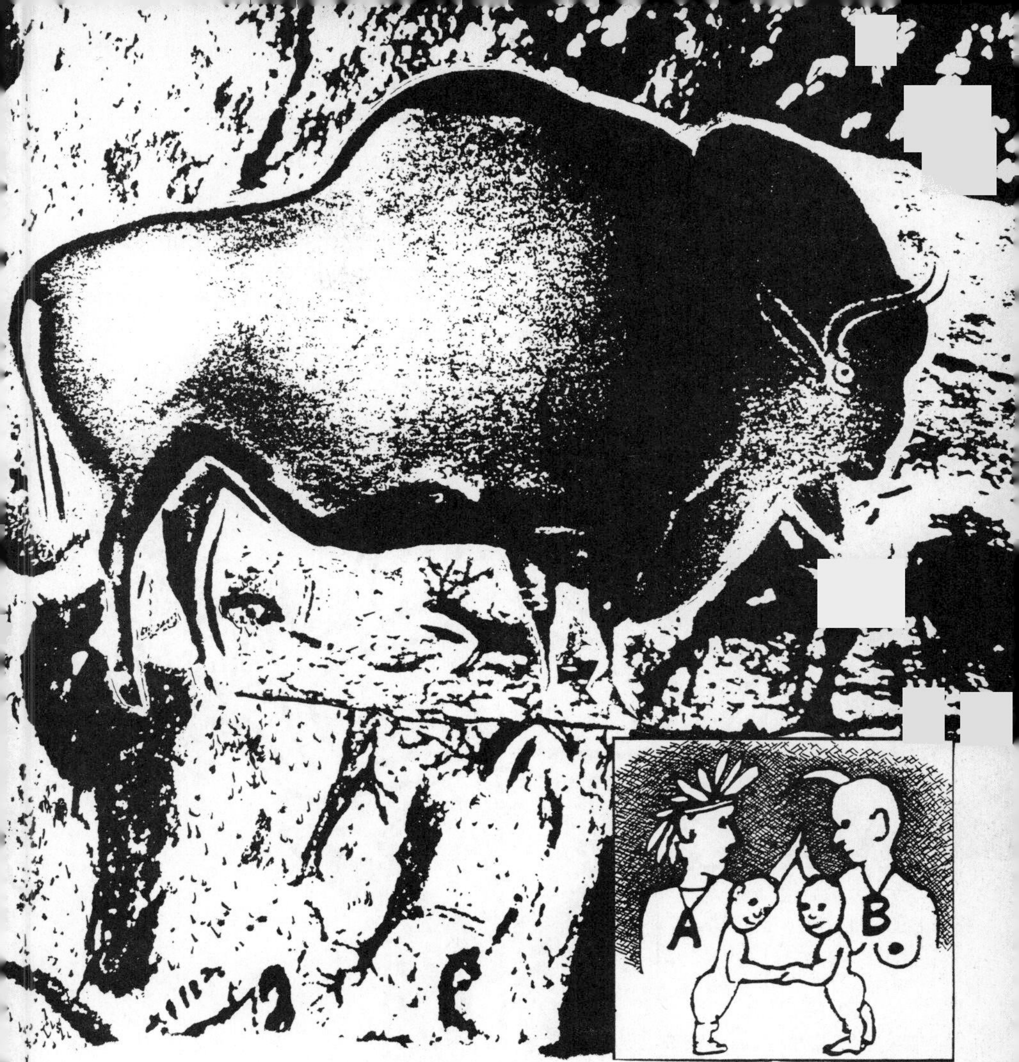

"Before the emergence of the incest taboo, culture does not exist; with its emergence, nature ceases to exist, for man, as the only kingdom. The prohibition of incest is the process by which nature goes beyond itself, it lights the spark which gives birth to a new and more complex type of structure, which superimposes itself upon the more elementary structures of mental life while integrating them, just as these structures superimpose themselves upon and integrate the yet more elementary structures of animal life. It brings about, and in itself constitutes, the advent of a new order." [CL-S]

Culture is a fire atop nature, set alight by the "spark" of the incest taboo.

TOTEMISM

Towards the end of the 19th century, anthropologists became very interested in the puzzle of **totemism**.

Totemism is the practice of symbolically associating a social group, such as a clan or lineage, with a particular kind of animal or plant (or, more rarely, with natural phenomena, such as lightning, or indeed any other kind of object, from rope to the bark of a tree).

THE TOTEMIC ANIMAL BECOMES AN HEREDITARY EMBLEM OR BADGE OF THE GROUP WHICH IS NAMED AFTER IT.

Totemism was first discovered at the end of the 18th century by an English merchant and interpreter called Long.

The term itself is derived from the vocabulary of the Ojibwa, an Amerindian tribe from the region of the North American Great Lakes.

Ojibwa society was divided into five main clans, in turn divided into smaller groups each named after an animal species – the totems. The five clans with their sub-groups were . . .

1. **Fish**: spirit of the waters, silurid, pike, sturgeon, salmon
2. **Crane**: eagle, sparrowhawk
3. **Diver**: seagull, cormorant, wild goose

4. **Bear**: wolf, lynx
5. **Moose**: marten, reindeer, beaver

What had particularly caught the imagination of the first anthropologists to tackle the puzzle of totemism was the mystical relationship that appeared to link the individuals of a group with the totemic animal. These animals were thought to be ancestrally or fraternally linked to the clans named after them.

KILLING OR EATING THE ANIMAL WAS OFTEN CONSIDERED TO BE TABOO.
SUCH PROHIBITIONS WERE TAKEN TO BE CHARACTERISTIC OF TOTEMISM IN GENERAL, ALTHOUGH NUMEROUS CASES DIDN'T FIT THE PICTURE.

Durkheim, writing in 1912, saw in totemism an early form of religion.

The fascination with totemism was to have a short life. Why, then, did Lévi-Strauss return to it?

THE RISE AND FALL OF TOTEMISM

The first to formulate a general theory of totemism in 1870 was an Edinburgh lawyer called **J.F. McLennan** (1827–81). In 1910, **J.G. Frazer** (1854–1941) published his monumental four-volume *Totemism and Exogamy*. This was followed in 1913 by Freud's *Totem and Taboo*, inspired by Frazer's work, which related totemism to his theory of the murder of the primeval father and the Oedipal phantasy underlying it.

THE INJUNCTIONS NOT TO KILL THE TOTEMIC ANIMAL OR TO MARRY WITHIN THE TOTEMIC GROUP ARE NEGATIONS OF THE OEDIPAL WISH TO KILL ONE'S FATHER AND MARRY ONE'S MOTHER.
FRAZER

By the 1920s, however, interest in the subject was dwindling. The study published that year by the French sociologist **Arnold van Gennep** (1873–1957) turned out to be one of the last book-length treatments of the subject, until Lévi-Strauss returned to it in 1962. In the 1930s and 40s, standard textbooks written by some of anthropology's greatest figures, such as Lowie, Kroeber and Boas, hardly mention the subject at all.

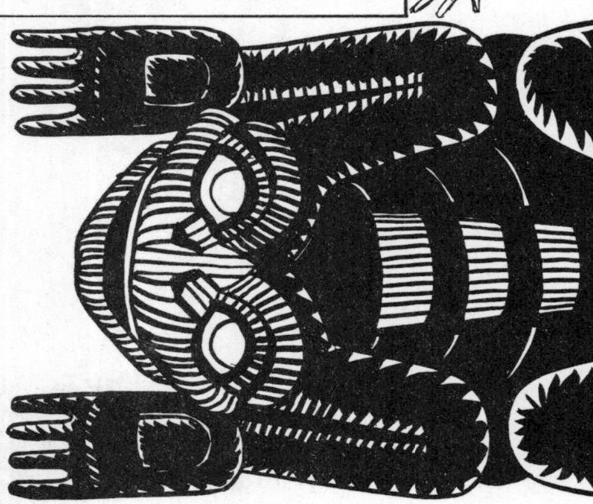
From the outset it was the problem of defining precisely what totemism is that constituted the principal stumbling-block for anthropologists.

Early theories on the question had been criticized for arbitrarily linking together disparate elements that could not be shown to be constitutive of totemism as such.

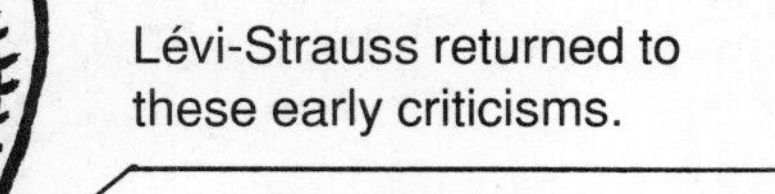

Lévi-Strauss returned to these early criticisms.

Totemism is a figment of the anthropologist's imagination, a projection. There is no totemism, but a "totemic illusion". What is the significance of this illusion?

He saw an intimate relationship between the kinds of theories that were developed at the turn of the century about totemism and those that were developed about **hysteria**.

TOTEMISM AND HYSTERIA

In a similar way that totemism was created by arbitrarily assembling a bundle of unrelated customs and beliefs, what was identified as hysteria in the psychiatric institutions of the late 19th century was also essentially a conglomerate of arbitrarily assembled symptoms.

AND IT WAS IN THE SAME CULTURAL MILIEU AND AT THE SAME EPOCH THAT TOTEMISM AND HYSTERIA **BOTH** BECAME FASHIONABLE.

In typifying certain groups of individuals either as totemic worshippers or as "hysterics", what unconsciously motivated the thinkers of the late 19th century was a desire to see the savage and the mentally ill patient as more **different** from themselves than they actually were.

THEIR THEORIES WERE ROUND-ABOUT WAYS OF DEALING WITH UNWANTED PARTS OF THE SELF, WHICH THE PRIMITIVE AND THE HYSTERIC EMBODIED.

By this means, scientists rejected certain modes of thought (seemingly irrational or incoherent) outside their own moral universe.

THAT'S WHAT I CAME TO REALIZE. THE DIFFERENCES BETWEEN MENTAL ILLNESS AND NORMAL PSYCHIC FUNCTIONING ARE ***QUANTITATIVE*** *RATHER THAN QUALITATIVE.*

EXCLUDING AND CLASSIFYING

What these early theories of totemism and hysteria did was to give a **natural basis** to the differences that were believed to set apart the sane from the mentally ill, the civilized from the savage.

In the same way, Lévi-Strauss reminds us, the painter **El Greco** (1541–1614) was excluded and classified as "unnatural".

Critics of El Greco preferred to believe that the strange elongated figures that he painted were the result of a malformation of the artist's eyeball, rather than the expression of a new and unique vision of the world.

The unstated reason why totemic theories emphasized the close relationship that was thought to link an individual to the totem animal was that it provided the scientific establishment with a convenient way of classifying cultures – here, in terms of their attitude *vis-à-vis* the natural world.

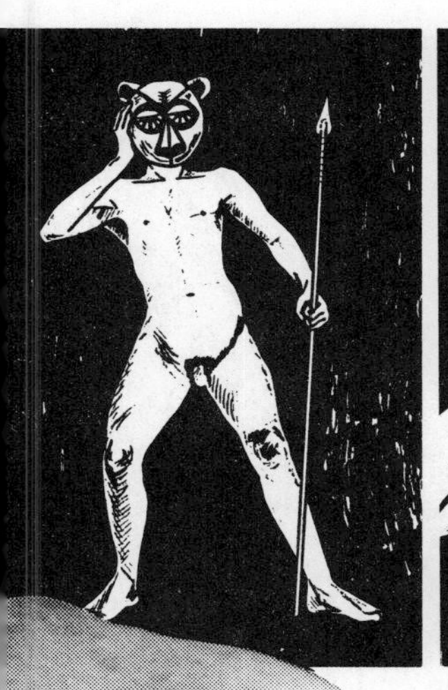

Totemism (as a theory) is first of all the projection outside of our world, and as if by an act of exorcism, of mental attitudes that are incompatible with the need - essential to Christian thought - to see man as separate from nature.

By attributing to the "savage" a whole system of animalistic identifications, from which Western man was presented as being exempt, the theory of totemism offered the means of distinguishing, within culture, between the civilized and the savage.

HOW IS "TOTEMISM" EXPLAINED?

Lévi-Strauss developed his own theory to explain "totemism". He came to see it as simply one aspect of a more widespread type of activity whose nature and purpose he was to analyze in great depth: **classification**.

He propounded that there is no "mystical" relationship between the individual and his totemic animal.

Totemism is a CODE, a symbolic language whose purpose is to signify SOCIAL DIFFERENCES. It is an instrument used by primitive populations for the classification of social groups.
What a society is expressing through totemism is something along these lines.
THE DIFFERENCES BETWEEN CLAN A AND CLAN B ARE THE SAME AS THE DIFFERENCES BETWEEN JAGUAR AND BEAR.
B
A
ONE MAY TRANSLATE THIS, FOR EXAMPLE, AS: THEY ARE BOTH CLANS OF HUNTERS, BUT THEY ARE NOT IN COMPETITION.

Totemism is a kind of elaborate metaphor. Through it, a society describes itself – its institutions and social structures. How does this metaphor work?

Natural species, in their great diversity, present the image of a vast system of **differences**.

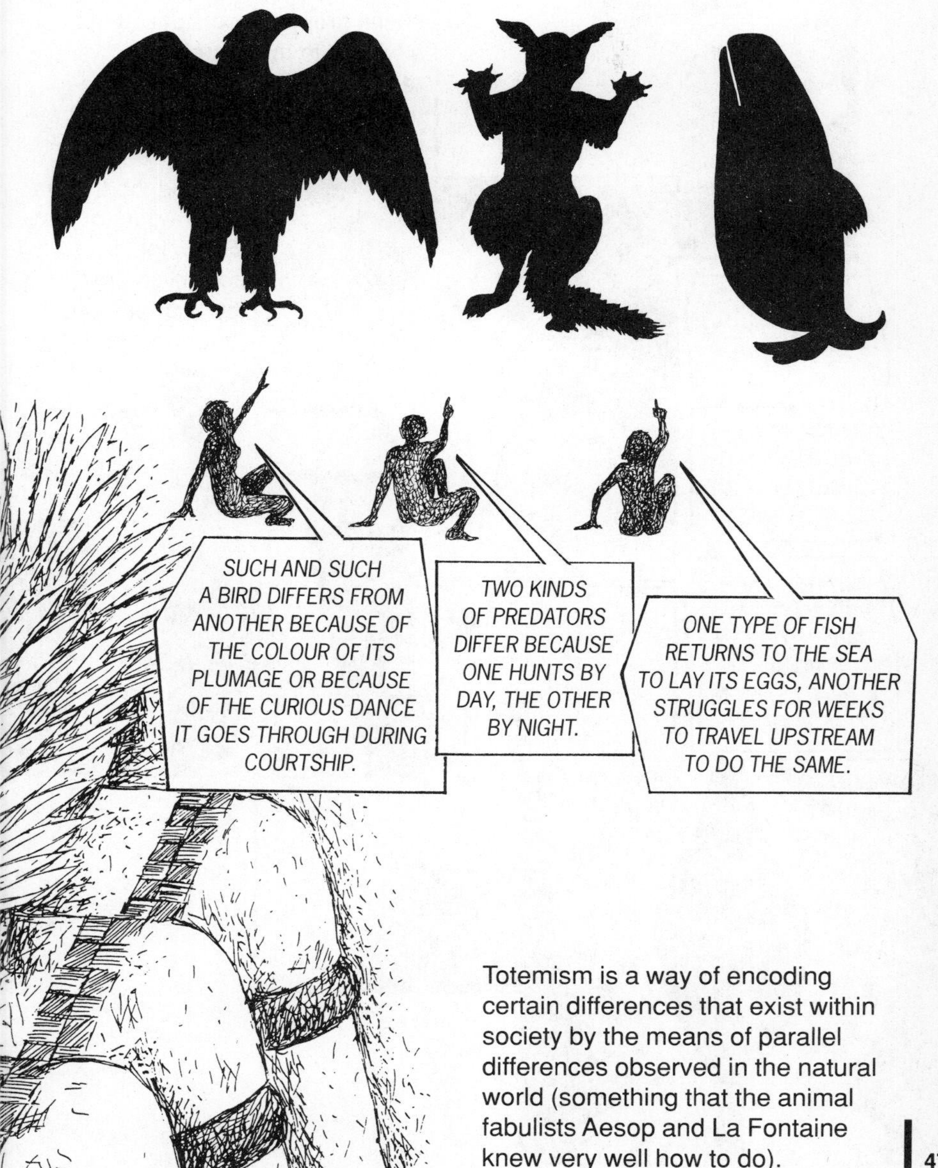

SUCH AND SUCH A BIRD DIFFERS FROM ANOTHER BECAUSE OF THE COLOUR OF ITS PLUMAGE OR BECAUSE OF THE CURIOUS DANCE IT GOES THROUGH DURING COURTSHIP.
TWO KINDS OF PREDATORS DIFFER BECAUSE ONE HUNTS BY DAY, THE OTHER BY NIGHT.
ONE TYPE OF FISH RETURNS TO THE SEA TO LAY ITS EGGS, ANOTHER STRUGGLES FOR WEEKS TO TRAVEL UPSTREAM TO DO THE SAME.

Totemism is a way of encoding certain differences that exist within society by the means of parallel differences observed in the natural world (something that the animal fabulists Aesop and La Fontaine knew very well how to do).

THE TOTEMIC OPERATOR

In totemism, the system of relationships that exists between social groups is **compared**, as a whole, to the system of relationships that exists between the various animals or plants after which the groups are named.

Among the Osage, neighbours of the Sioux Indians, a totemic animal may be dismembered and reassembled.

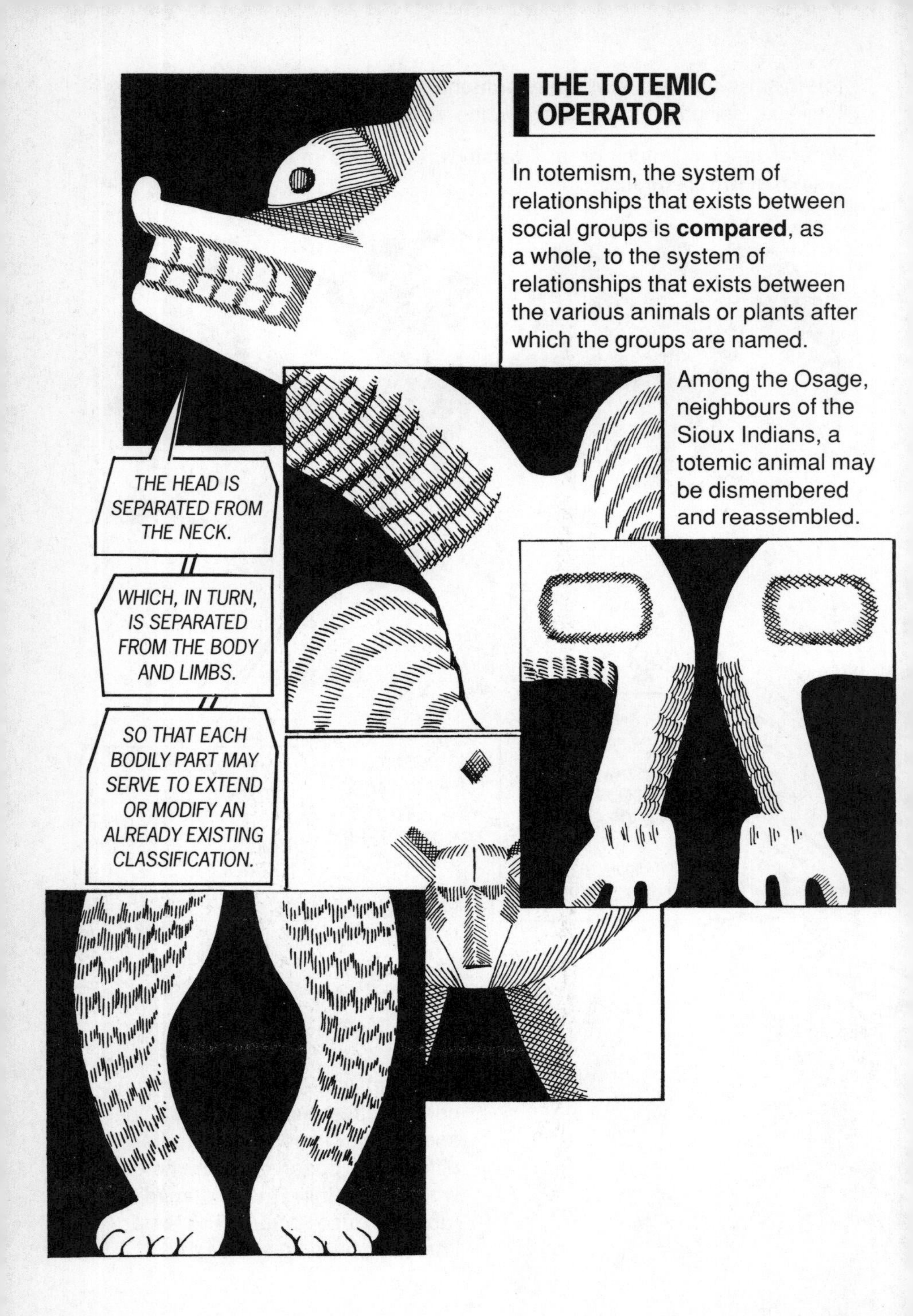
THE HEAD IS SEPARATED FROM THE NECK.
WHICH, IN TURN, IS SEPARATED FROM THE BODY AND LIMBS.
SO THAT EACH BODILY PART MAY SERVE TO EXTEND OR MODIFY AN ALREADY EXISTING CLASSIFICATION.

For the same purpose, elements from one animal may be combined with those from other similarly rearranged animal species.

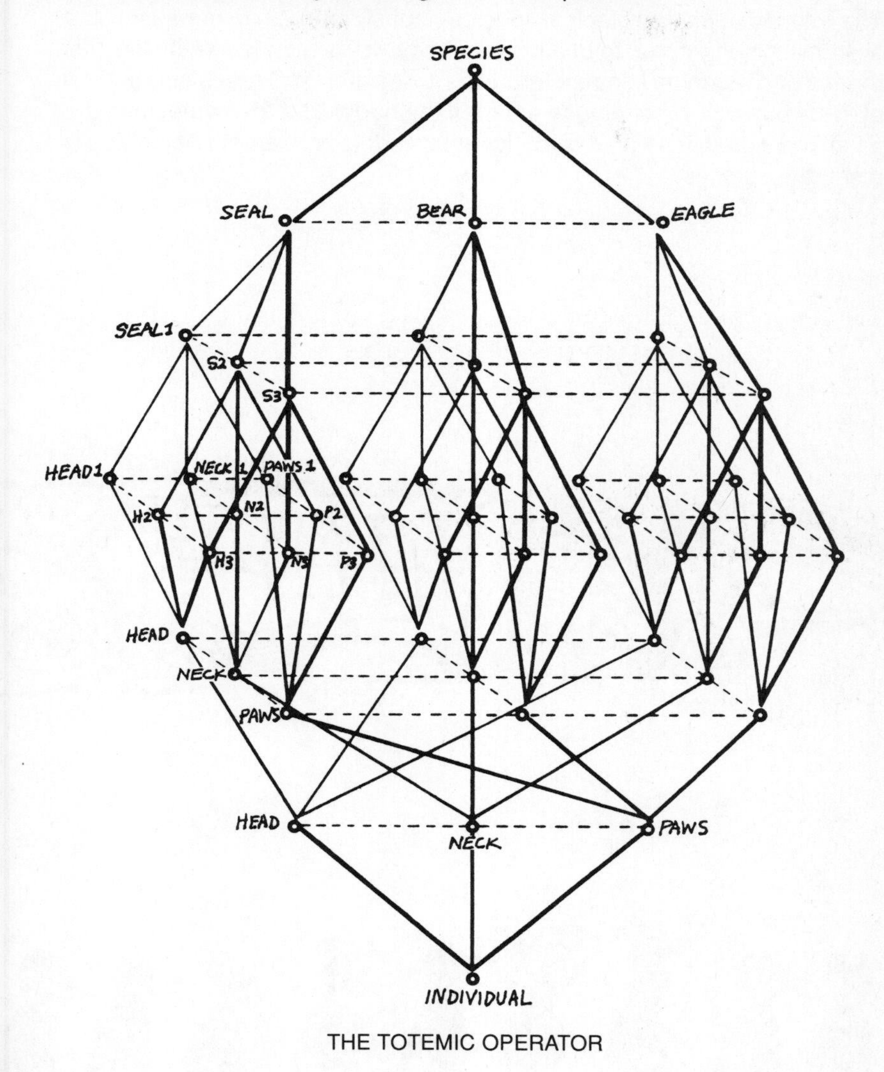
SPECIES
SEAL
BEAR
EAGLE
SEAL1
S2
S3
HEAD1
NECK 1
PAWS 1
H2
N2
P2
H3
N3
P3
HEAD
NECK
PAWS
HEAD
NECK
PAWS
INDIVIDUAL

THE TOTEMIC OPERATOR

Thus, in totemism the animal (or plant) may be used as a kind of multi-purpose symbolic tool to "de-totalize" or "re-totalize" any entity. What are the classificatory purposes of these "surgical" operations?

The key lies in the dynamic inherent to the very notion of **species**.

SPECIES AND SYSTEMS

The totemic animal (biological species), considered as an organism, is a system in itself (made up of a head, a body, limbs etc.). As such, it is the means of conceptualizing the group as a social "body" (each sub-division of the group corresponding to a part of the body). But the same animal, as an individual, may also be conceptualized as an element belonging to a set (the species).

This set or species is made up of a theoretically infinite number of same elements (all bears, all eagles). Thus, the "totemic operator" may be used either to conceptualize a community made up of a multitude of social groups (each corresponding to the individuals that make up a species), or a social group that is like a complex organism.

THE TOTEMIC ANIMAL IS A LOGICAL TOOL FOR CONCEPTUALIZING RELATIONSHIPS BETWEEN GROUPS AND RELATIONSHIPS BETWEEN INDIVIDUALS AND GROUPS.

THE NATURE OF THINKING

Lévi-Strauss thought that the early theories of totemism got the ethnographic data all wrong. But more fundamentally, his whole approach to the subject reflects a very different understanding of the nature of the so-called "primitive mind". His analysis reveals the hidden **logic** at work in totemism.

The complicated and sometimes strange nomenclature of totemism is the expression of a concealed yet totally coherent SYMBOLIC SYSTEM.

This is important because one of the major aims of Lévi-Strauss's anthropology is to demonstrate that the **fundamental mental operations** that determine the way we think are the same all over the world, and have remained unchanged throughout the whole of man's history as a speaking member of human society.

The basic dictum that has guided Lévi-Strauss throughout his inquiries into the world of primitive man is: *l'homme a toujours pensé aussi bien* – man has always thought equally well. What **have** changed are the kinds of things to which we have applied our minds.

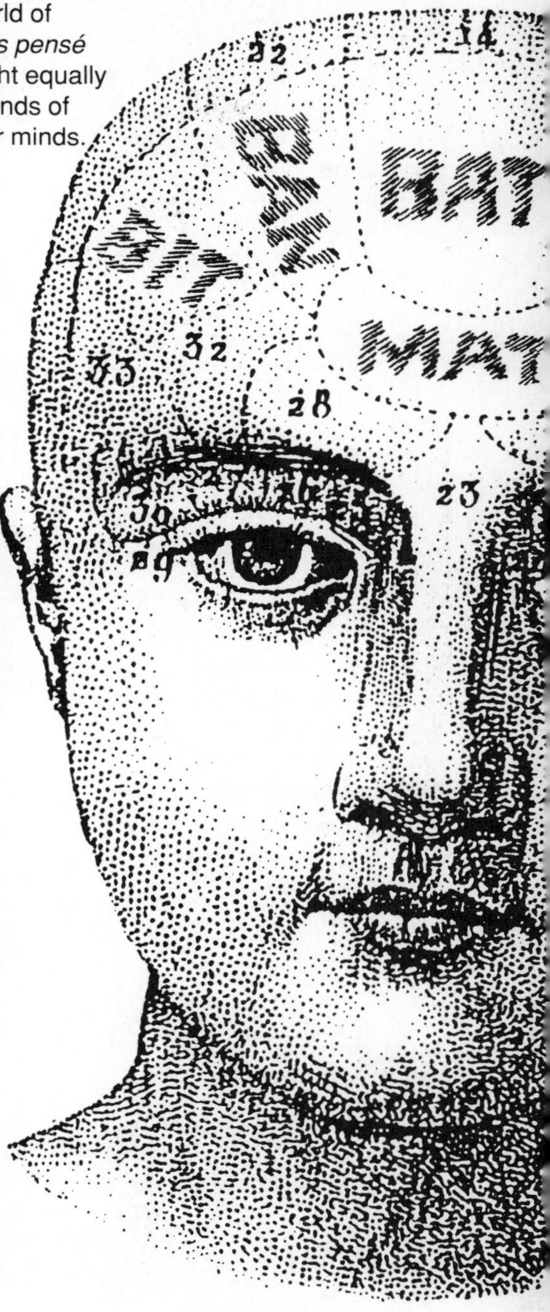

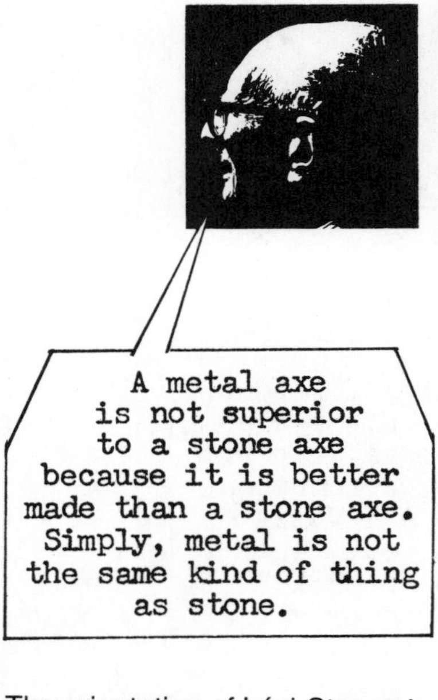

A metal axe is not superior to a stone axe because it is better made than a stone axe. Simply, metal is not the same kind of thing as stone.

The orientation of Lévi-Strauss's anthropology may conveniently be presented in terms of an opposition, on the one hand with Lucien Lévy-Bruhl, and on the other with Malinowski.

THE INSTINCT FOR KNOWLEDGE

Lucien Lévy-Bruhl (1857–1939), one of Lévi-Strauss's eminent predecessors, relegated primitive populations to a world of pre-logical, pre-scientific thought.

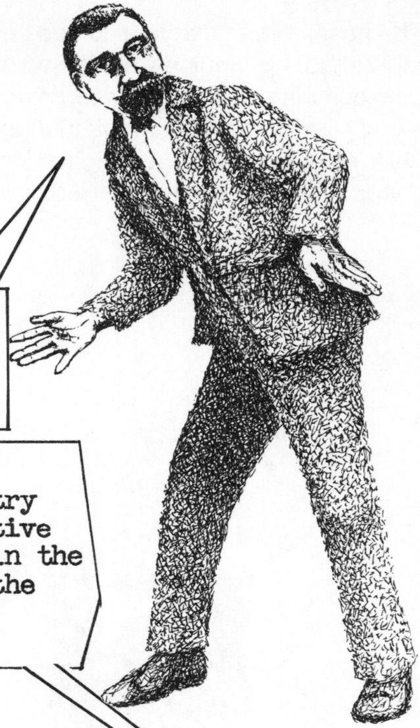

THEY ARE DOMINATED BY AFFECTIVITY AND A SENSE OF "MYSTICAL" PARTICIPATION WITH THE NATURAL WORLD.

In opposition to Lévy-Bruhl, I try to show that primitive thinking is logical in the same sense and in the same manner as our own.

Malinowski developed the utilitarian idea that primitive thought is entirely determined by the basic needs of life.

PLANT SPECIES ARE KNOWN ONLY IN AS MUCH AS THEY ARE EDIBLE.

To this, I retort that plant species (as we have seen with totemism) are not only "BONNES À MANGER" - good to eat, but "BONNES À PENSER" - good to think with.

Against Malinowski, Lévi-Strauss demonstrates that primitive man is capable of disinterested knowledge. Lévi-Strauss paints a portrait of primitive man absorbed in the task of trying to understand the natural world that he perceives around him.

THIS I DO PRINCIPALLY THROUGH ACTS OF CLASSIFICATION – BY CREATING OPPOSITIONS, BY DIFFERENTIATING ELEMENTS, IN A WORD, BY CREATING ***ORDER****.*

And what drives primitive man in these tasks is a **will to knowledge** that has no other end than its own fulfilment, a kind of "instinct for knowledge".

ANTHROPOLOGY IS A PSYCHOLOGY

Lévi-Strauss's ideas about the nature of the "primitive mind" go hand in hand with his redefinition of the goals of anthropology, to which he gave a cognitive twist. How is this?

As **J.G. Merquior** (b. 1941), a former member of Lévi-Strauss's élite seminar held at the Collège de France, has put it: Lévi-Strauss stands Durkheim on his head.

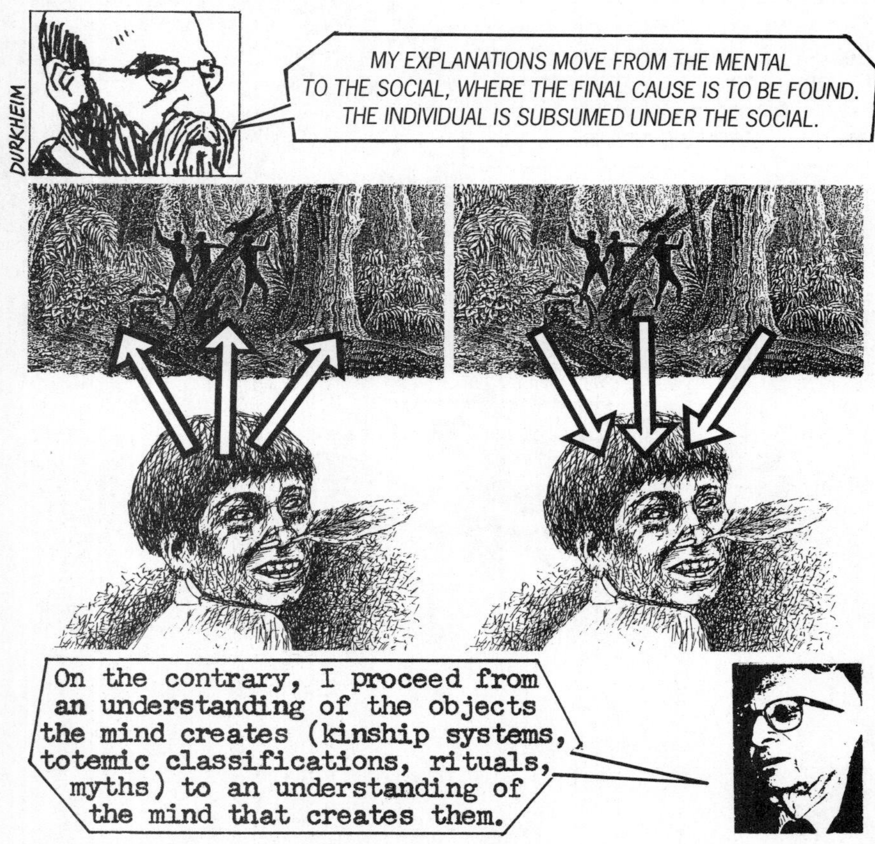
DURKHEIM
MY EXPLANATIONS MOVE FROM THE MENTAL TO THE SOCIAL, WHERE THE FINAL CAUSE IS TO BE FOUND. THE INDIVIDUAL IS SUBSUMED UNDER THE SOCIAL.
On the contrary, I proceed from an understanding of the objects the mind creates (kinship systems, totemic classifications, rituals, myths) to an understanding of the mind that creates them.

For Lévi-Strauss, "anthropology is primarily a psychology" concerned with the mind's structural functioning. This has been his constant theme. "Throughout, my intention remains the same: starting from ethnographic experience, I have always aimed at drawing up an inventory of mental patterns, to reduce apparently arbitrary data to some kind of order, and to attain a level at which a kind of necessity becomes apparent, underlying the illusions of freedom." [CL-S]

CLASSIFICATION OR TAXONOMY

Lévi-Strauss's ideas about the so-called "primitive mentality", which he shows is not primitive in any derogatory sense, form the background to the book he published in 1962, one of his most complex and challenging works: *La Pensée sauvage*. (The English title, *The Savage Mind*, for reasons that will become apparent, is misleading.) When it first came out it created a tremendous stir, as much among philosophers as among anthropologists. That year a special edition of the philosophical journal *Esprit* was devoted to Lévi-Strauss. These were, until 1966, the years of Structuralism's glory.

La Pensée sauvage opens with some remarks and examples . . .

- The vocabulary of the Chinook tribe from the Northwest coast of North America and their use of abstract words.
- The names of planets in observatories.
- The names of horses on merry-go-rounds.
- The number of terms the Fang from Gabon possess to designate animal species.

The problem I introduce in this way, around which all others revolve in LA PENSÉE SAUVAGE, is that of classification.
STAR
SPIRIT
FLAME

La Pensée sauvage is a study of the methods of classification of primitive cultures. It is a book about **taxonomy**.

La Pensée sauvage follows on from his work on totemism: a study of the total system of which totemism is but a part. And it goes further than that. Through his study of primitive systems of classification, Lévi-Strauss brings to light and describes the functioning of a timeless "wild" mode of thought, or *pensée sauvage*.

What is so important about classification?

> At stake in my attempt to understand classificatory systems (more precisely, to understand cultural practices AS classification) is the question of how man relates to his immediate environment.

La Pensée sauvage is concerned with how primitive man uses elements of his perceptual experience to construct symbolic systems, among them, and above all, systems of classification. Classificatory systems are conceptual schemas that enable man to apprehend the natural and social world as organized totalities.

The Pawnee Indians celebrate seasonal rites in a purpose-built hut, the posts of which are made from different types of wood selected according to where they will be positioned.
EACH POST IS PAINTED IN A COLOUR ASSOCIATED SYMBOLICALLY WITH A GEOGRAPHICAL ORIENTATION . . .
. . . WHICH, IN TURN, IS ASSOCIATED WITH ONE OF THE FOUR SEASONS THAT TOGETHER FORM THE CALENDAR YEAR.
THESE ASSOCIATIONS ARE NOT ARBITRARY, BUT FORM A COMPLETE CLASSIFICATORY SYSTEM, A CONCEPTUAL SCHEMA THAT REPRESENTS THE UNIVERSE AS A CONTINUUM AND MEDIATES BETWEEN THE NOTIONS OF SPACE AND TIME.
poplar..........white...... south-west
south.....summer
box-elder.....red......... south-east
SPACE
year TIME
elm..............black...... north-east
north.....winter
willow..........yellow.....north-west

Classificatory systems extend like a net over nature and social reality. Through them, the world is inscribed in a structured ensemble, a network of symbolic relationships which transforms the world into an organized totality.

The Navajo recognize two types of beings, those which possess speech and those which do not. Among the beings that don't are animals and plants.

ANIMALS ARE DISTINGUISHED ACCORDING TO WHETHER THEY RUN, FLY OR CRAWL.
WITHIN THESE THREE CATEGORIES, TWO FURTHER DISTINCTIONS ARE MADE: FIRST, BETWEEN ANIMALS THAT TRAVEL ON LAND AND ANIMALS THAT TRAVEL OVER WATER.
AND SECOND, BETWEEN ANIMALS THAT TRAVEL BY NIGHT AND ANIMALS THAT TRAVEL BY DAY.

Within this classificatory schema every living being finds its rightful place.

A native thinker once remarked: "All sacred things must have their place." To which Lévi-Strauss has added: being in their place is what makes them sacred.

SOME PROPERTIES OF CLASSIFICATORY SYSTEMS

1. Interconnectedness

One striking feature of classificatory systems is that they link up to form vast conceptual networks. Each classificatory system does not exist in isolation but is related to many others according to complex symbolic correspondences and relationships of transformation. An example.

The Dogon from Sudan recognize 22 main plant families, some of which are divided into 11 sub-groups. The 22 families, when listed in the correct order, make up two series: an odd series and an even series.

IN THE FIRST SERIES, WHICH SYMBOLIZES BIRTHS OF SINGLE CHILDREN, MALE AND FEMALE PLANTS ARE RESPECTIVELY ASSOCIATED WITH THE RAINY SEASON AND THE DRY SEASON.
IN THE SECOND SERIES, WHICH SYMBOLIZES BIRTHS OF TWINS, THE SAME ASSOCIATION EXISTS (MALE/FEMALE, RAINY/DRY), BUT REVERSED.

Each plant family is separated into three categories: trees, shrubs and grass. Finally, each family is associated with a part of the body, a technique, a social class and an institution.

2. Extendability

Classificatory systems possess a virtually unlimited capacity to expand while still maintaining their inner coherence. This may occur in two separate directions.

Downwards

On the one hand, the mesh of the classificatory net may contract. Classification becomes increasingly concrete and evolves towards the particular (this is the **analytic** pole of the system). Classifications based on animal and plant species are characteristic of this end of the classificatory system which mobilizes a rich lexicon of classificatory terms.

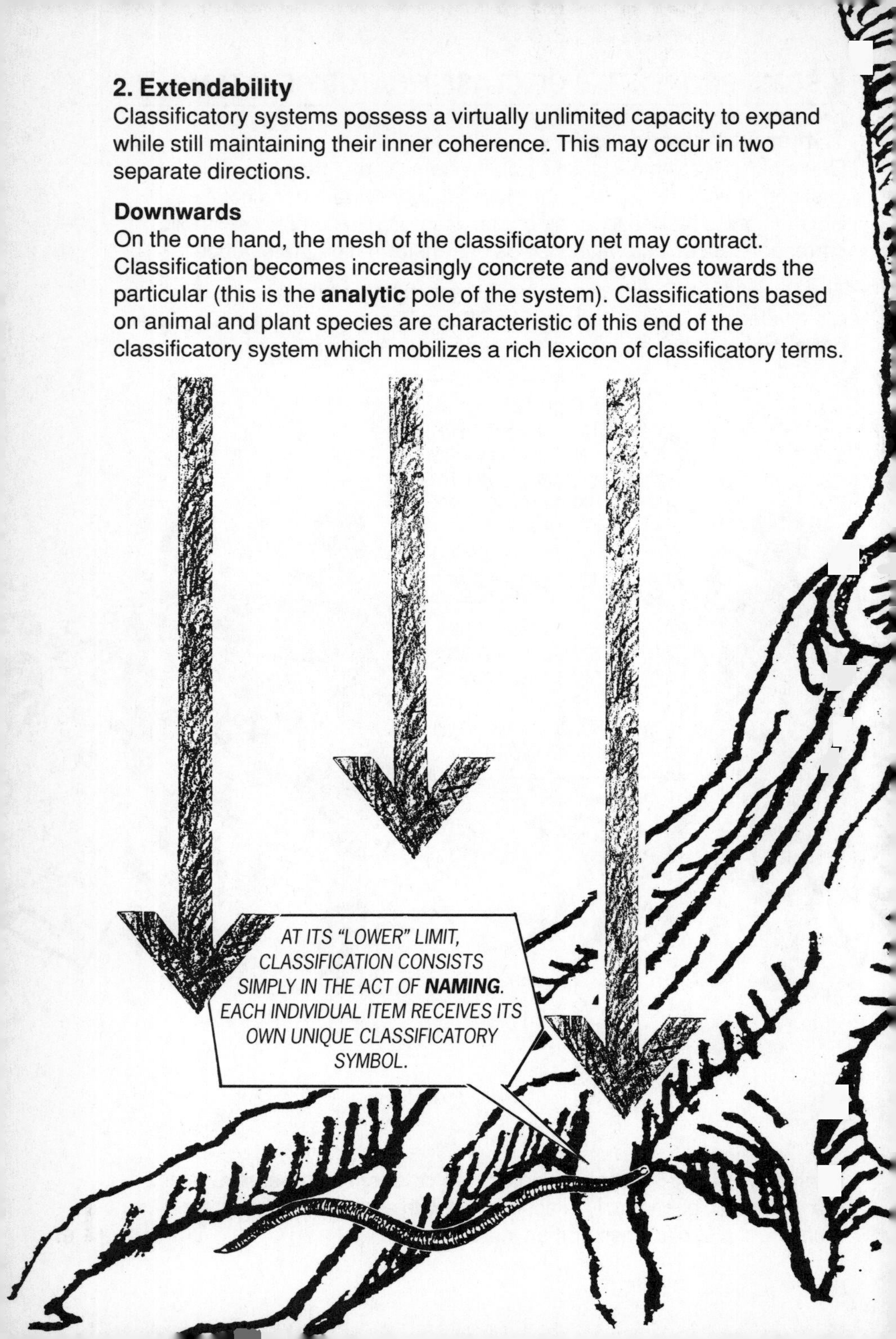

AT ITS "LOWER" LIMIT, CLASSIFICATION CONSISTS SIMPLY IN THE ACT OF **NAMING**. EACH INDIVIDUAL ITEM RECEIVES ITS OWN UNIQUE CLASSIFICATORY SYMBOL.

Upwards
On the other hand, the net of the classificatory system may expand. Here, classification evolves towards abstraction (the **synthetic** pole of the system) to the point where all things are included in a simple logical opposition – for example, a black and white opposition of the type that characterizes the famous Yin and Yang emblem.

AT THIS END OF THE SYSTEM, CLASSIFIERS MAY COME TO INCLUDE SUCH THINGS AS NUMBERS, CARDINAL POINTS OR PRIMARY COLOURS.

Each classificatory system, unlike the reality it encapsulates, is made up of a finite number of discrete elements. It is the means of a reconstruction of the real, at the level of the symbol, into a signifying whole.

WHAT IS THINKING?

Lévi-Strauss came to see the classificatory systems that he studied as one expression of a *pensée sauvage* which he postulated to be at work at the very heart of culture. This gives the measure of the ambition of his theory. Through his analysis of classificatory systems, what Lévi-Strauss is getting at is the description of an independent and autonomous **mode of thought**.

So the implications of what Lévi-Strauss was arguing for did not only concern anthropologists; he challenged the conceptions of all those who made thinking their business.

Jacques Lacan (1901–81), for example, in his famous seminar *The Four Fundamental Concepts of Psycho-Analysis* (1964) held at the Ecole Normale Supérieure, was led to ask . . .

LA PENSÉE SAUVAGE, WHICH LÉVI-STRAUSS PLACES AT THE BASIS OF THE STATUTES OF SOCIETY, IS ONE UNCONSCIOUS, BUT IS IT ENOUGH TO ACCOMMODATE THE UNCONSCIOUS AS SUCH?

What does Lévi-Strauss mean by *pensée sauvage*?

The title of his book relies on a pun: *pensées* in French are at once thoughts and a kind of flower – a **wild** flower, *Viola tricolor* (a pansy). So it is not so much "untamed" thought as "untouched" thought. It is thinking in the wild. And there is nothing "*sauvage*" about it. On the contrary, it is rigorous, systematic, organized.

Lévi-Strauss quotes from the novelist **Honoré de Balzac** (1799–1850).

THOUGHTS MAKE UP IN MAN A COMPLETE SYSTEM, LIKE ONE OF NATURE'S KINGDOMS, A KIND OF EFFLORESCENCE THE ICONOGRAPHY OF WHICH WILL ONE DAY BE DESCRIBED BY A MAN OF GENIUS WHO WILL PERHAPS BE TAKEN FOR MAD.

What Lévi-Strauss terms *pensée sauvage* is at once ancient and contemporary. His idea is that during the Neolithic era, which began in Europe around 10,000 or 12,000 years ago, it formed the basis of a primitive science to which we owe the invention of the principal arts and crafts of civilization, such as pottery, weaving, agriculture and the domestication of animals.

Although a new form of science emerged out of Greek culture, it never fully replaced its predecessor. *Sauvage* modes of thought continued to exist alongside others (in particular, what Lévi-Strauss calls "domesticated" or "cultivated" thought) which are in essence **specialized** modes of thought geared for productivity.

BUILDING BRIDGES.
SOLVING MATHEMATICAL EQUATIONS.
CALCULATING PROBABILITIES.

How does Lévi-Strauss's understanding of the nature of primitive science shed light on what *la pensée sauvage* is?

There exist two distinct modes of scientific thought: a modern science that emerged out of Greek culture and a much more ancient "*science sauvage*" with origins going far back in pre-Neolithic times. But these two modes of thought are not the result of an evolution (or a difference) in the way man thinks (since, according to Lévi-Strauss, "man has always thought equally well"). Rather, they correspond to the two strategic levels at which nature allows itself to be penetrated by scientific understanding: the first, directly adapted to **sensory perception**, the other, independent of it.

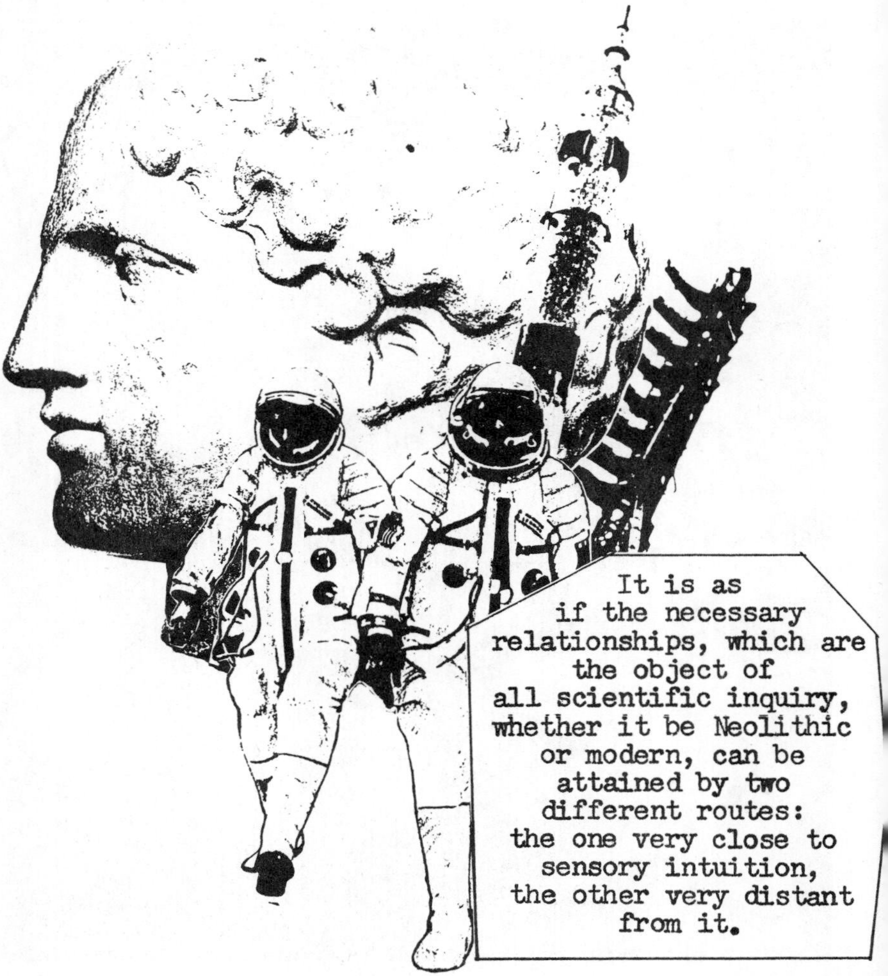

It is as if the necessary relationships, which are the object of all scientific inquiry, whether it be Neolithic or modern, can be attained by two different routes: the one very close to sensory intuition, the other very distant from it.

THE LOGIC OF THE CONCRETE

The particularity of *la pensée sauvage* (the basis of primitive science) is that it constructs its edifices directly out of the data of sense perception. It is a logic of sense perception or "logic of the concrete", as Lévi-Strauss sometimes calls it.

It is a mode of thought that is at once spontaneous and coherent, steeped in concrete images and, in its own way, a theoretical tool.

This mode of thought is rooted in what 17th century philosophers like **John Locke** (1632–1704) called "secondary qualities".

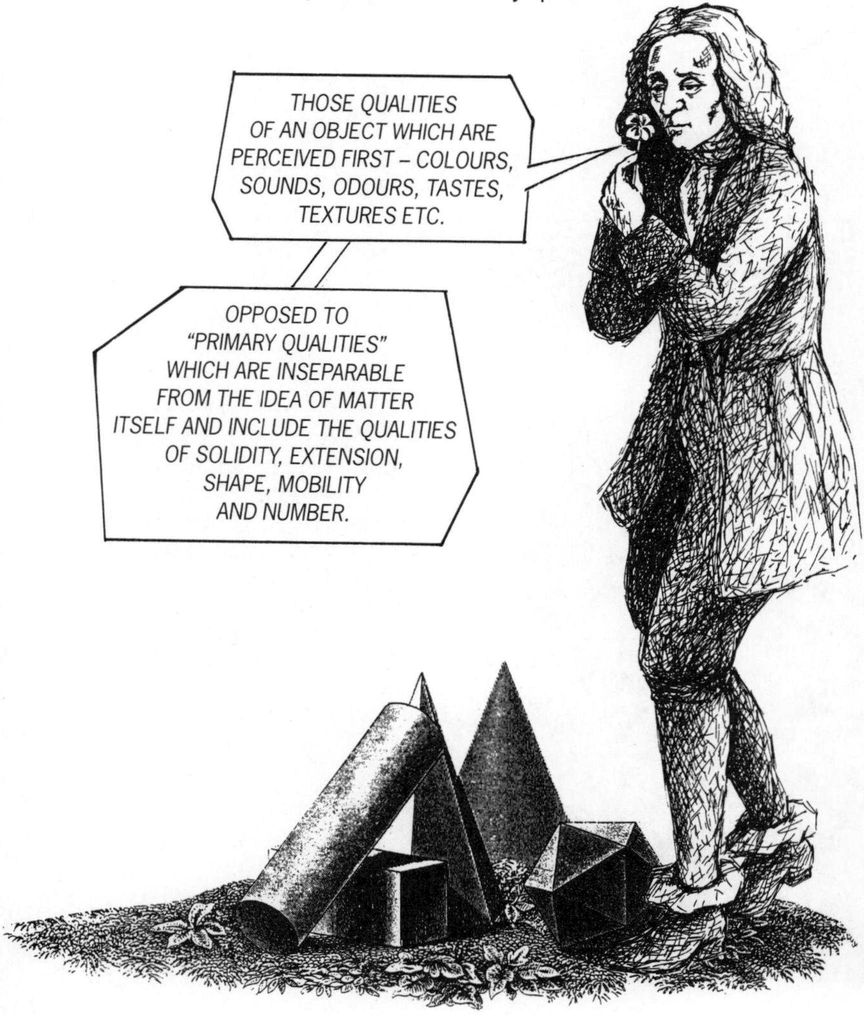

THOSE QUALITIES OF AN OBJECT WHICH ARE PERCEIVED FIRST – COLOURS, SOUNDS, ODOURS, TASTES, TEXTURES ETC.
OPPOSED TO "PRIMARY QUALITIES" WHICH ARE INSEPARABLE FROM THE IDEA OF MATTER ITSELF AND INCLUDE THE QUALITIES OF SOLIDITY, EXTENSION, SHAPE, MOBILITY AND NUMBER.

THINKING BY ANALOGIES

The logic of the concrete – what drives "wild thinking" – proceeds by directly cross-relating the data of sense perception in vast systems of **analogies**. Shapes, colours, tastes and any other observable features are all interrelated and used as the elements of a code.

In contrast with modern logic, there is no recourse to a plane of abstract formalization.

U
=
Concrete logic functions at a level of experience where logical properties manifest themselves as attributes of things as directly as flavours or perfumes.

A useful way of thinking about this is to relate it to the way in which certain works of art "talk to us" through the senses. If a lake in a painting evokes stillness, it is not because it symbolizes stillness or even "represents" it: stillness is *there*, immanent in the image of the lake. Lévi-Strauss himself invites the comparison with aesthetic experience.

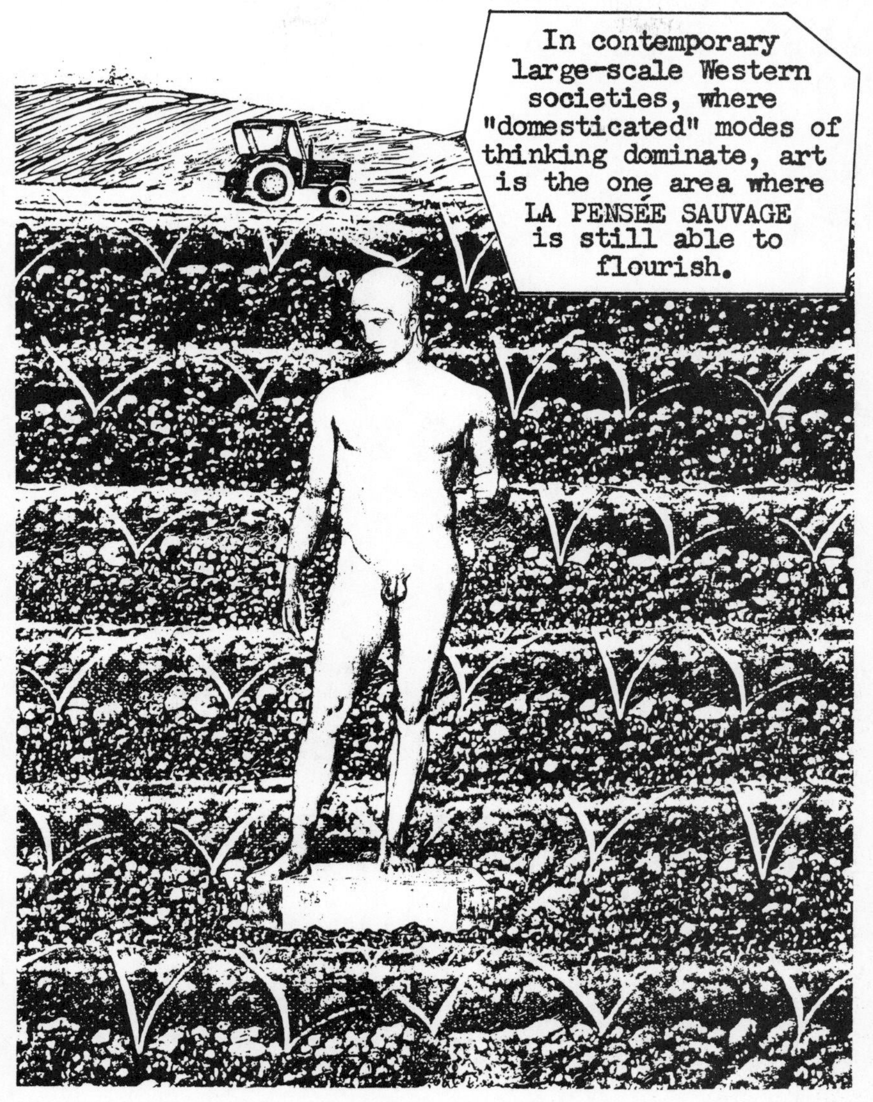
In contemporary large-scale Western societies, where "domesticated" modes of thinking dominate, art is the one area where LA PENSÉE SAUVAGE is still able to flourish.

For Lévi-Strauss, art in contemporary societies is the natural preserve of this "concrete logic" which is an aspect of *la pensée sauvage*.

HOW CONCRETE LOGIC FUNCTIONS

Concrete logic constructs organized systems directly out of the material of sensory experience. It selects from nature – which offers in this respect virtually limitless possibilities – certain distinctive features which it then renders operative within a given system.

In this respect, it follows the way in which natural languages function.

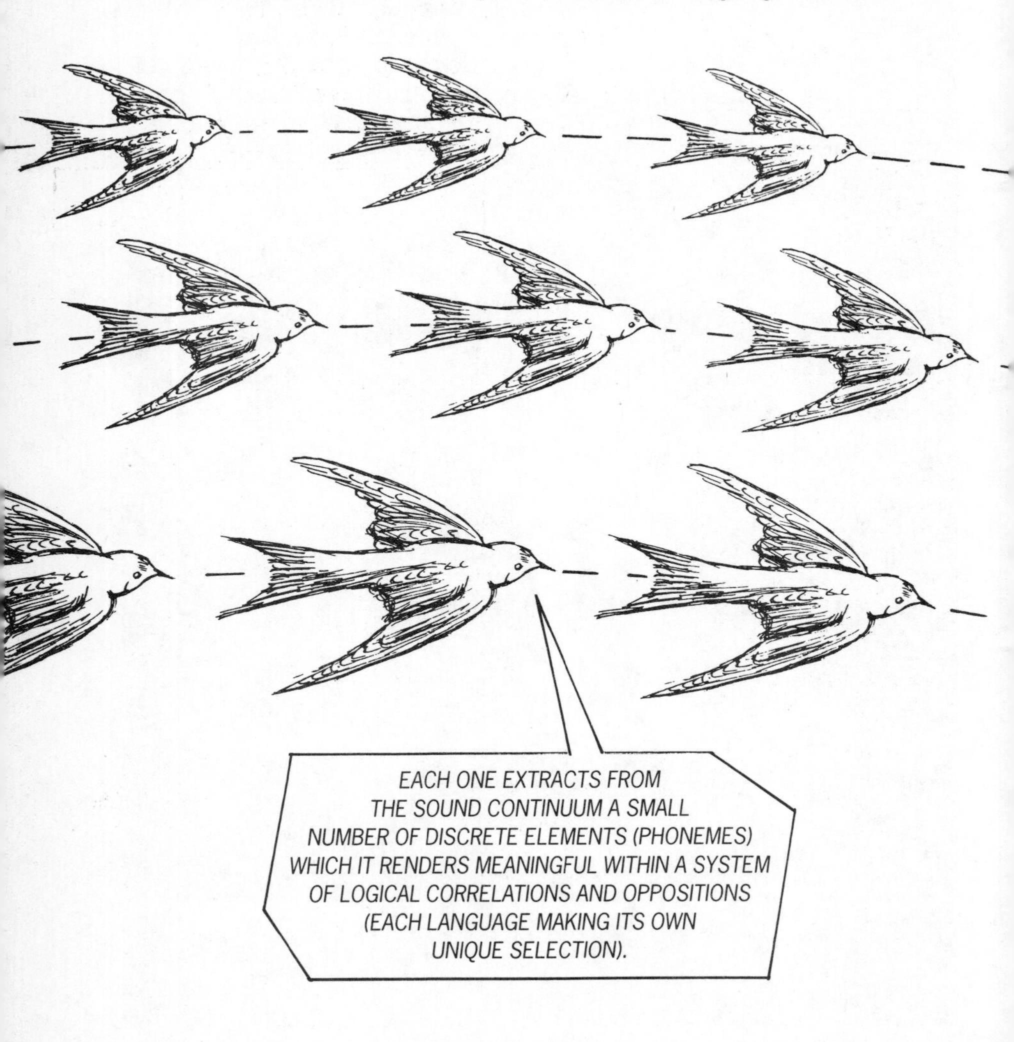
EACH ONE EXTRACTS FROM THE SOUND CONTINUUM A SMALL NUMBER OF DISCRETE ELEMENTS (PHONEMES) WHICH IT RENDERS MEANINGFUL WITHIN A SYSTEM OF LOGICAL CORRELATIONS AND OPPOSITIONS (EACH LANGUAGE MAKING ITS OWN UNIQUE SELECTION).

Let's see how the logic of the concrete functions in the divinatory system used by the Iban tribe of Southern Borneo.

The Iban construct a divinatory system out of the flight and song of seven birds, each selected for some special characteristic that it possesses.

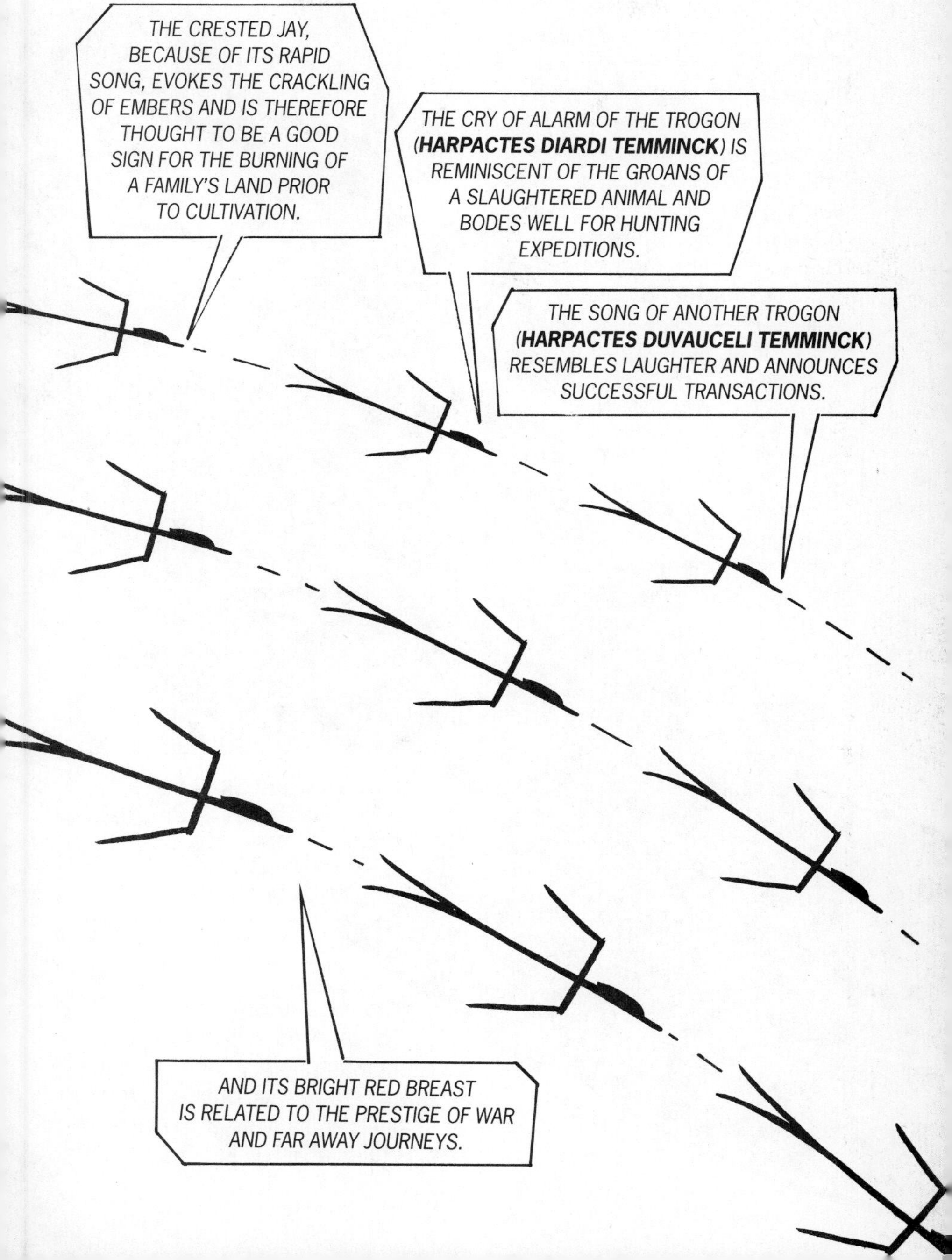

THE CRESTED JAY, BECAUSE OF ITS RAPID SONG, EVOKES THE CRACKLING OF EMBERS AND IS THEREFORE THOUGHT TO BE A GOOD SIGN FOR THE BURNING OF A FAMILY'S LAND PRIOR TO CULTIVATION.
THE CRY OF ALARM OF THE TROGON (**HARPACTES DIARDI TEMMINCK**) IS REMINISCENT OF THE GROANS OF A SLAUGHTERED ANIMAL AND BODES WELL FOR HUNTING EXPEDITIONS.
THE SONG OF ANOTHER TROGON (**HARPACTES DUVAUCELI TEMMINCK**) RESEMBLES LAUGHTER AND ANNOUNCES SUCCESSFUL TRANSACTIONS.
AND ITS BRIGHT RED BREAST IS RELATED TO THE PRESTIGE OF WAR AND FAR AWAY JOURNEYS.

At its simplest, concrete logic is to be understood as "the respect for and use of the data of the senses".

The philosopher **René Descartes** (1596–1650) is generally considered to have laid down the foundations of modern scientific thought in his *Discourse on the Method of Rightly Conducting Reason and Reaching the Truth in the Sciences* (1637), which set out what he thought should be the guiding principles of scientific inquiry.

MY METHOD IS TO DIVIDE ANY PROBLEM ANALYTICALLY INTO AS MANY PARTS AS ARE REQUIRED TO SOLVE IT. BY EXAMINING THE PARTS, ONE ARRIVES AT AN UNDERSTANDING OF THE WHOLE.

LA PENSÉE SAUVAGE, on the contrary, fulfils what is essentially a TOTALIZING ambition.

Where Cartesian logic divides, "wild thinking", like the metaphorical thinking that is characteristic of poetry, brings together. Its overriding concern is to establish links.

About "wild thinking" Lévi-Strauss writes: "Its aim is to reach by the shortest possible means a general understanding of the universe – and not only a general but a total understanding. That is, it is a way of thinking which must imply that if you don't understand everything, you don't explain anything."

HOW CAN SUCH A MODE OF THINKING BE EFFECTIVE AS A METHOD OF SCIENTIFIC INQUIRY?

I am not saying that primitive or "wild" science and modern science are equal in their results.

Lévi-Strauss shows that *at the level of understanding that is its own* (sense perception), primitive science can work. How can it work?

HOW PRIMITIVE SCIENCE WORKS

The primitive scientist makes inferences on the basis of the information of sense data alone. He understands intuitively that the observable properties of natural objects are the signs of other hidden properties. Although this understanding is not "scientific", it can order the world in a way that works, since the outer appearance of things reflects certain inner realities. The order in the natural world can thus be perceived through the senses, as by the poet and artist, as well as through scientific theorizing. Both are ways of understanding an object.

To prove his point, Lévi-Strauss appeals to our own sensory knowledge.

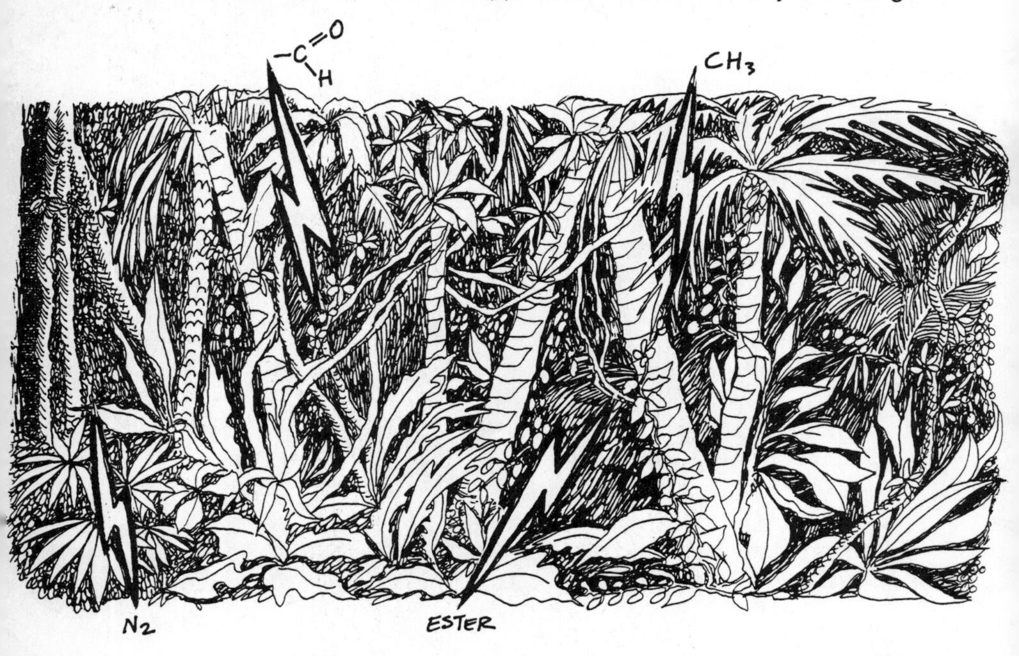
–C=O
H
CH3
N2
ESTER

Sensory information alone is enough to tell us that tobacco smoke is related, on the one hand, to grilled meat and the brown crust of bread, and on the other to cheese, beer and honey.

Modern science explains why: like the first group, tobacco smoke contains nitrogen, and like the second, diacetyl.

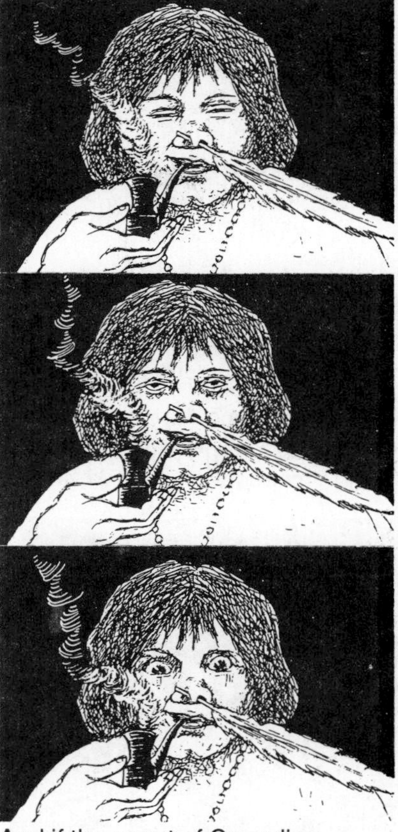

Similarly, our senses tell us that wild cherry, cinnamon, vanilla and sherry form a group; indeed, they all contain aldehyde.

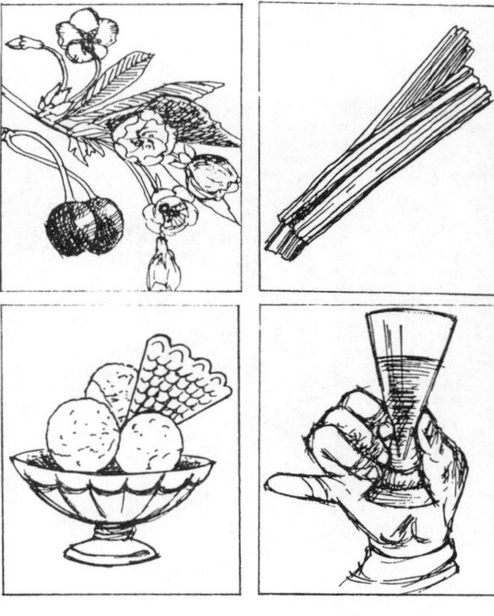

And if the scent of Canadian Wintergreen tea, lavender and banana seem similar, it is because of the presence in each of ester.

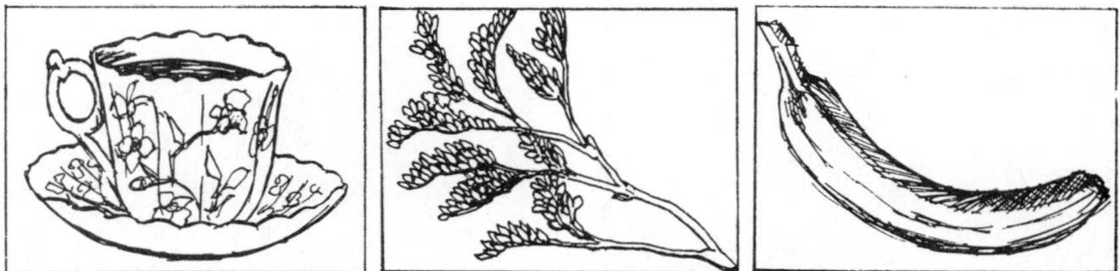

In other words, our sensory perception may at times be as good as a test tube for drawing certain conclusions about the world. In this hi-tech age, Lévi-Strauss reminds us that man can apprehend the world by different means. Science provides one way of understanding reality, and the "science of the concrete" another.

BRICOLAGE

To describe the functioning of this logic of the concrete – the essence of *la pensée sauvage* – Lévi-Strauss uses an unusual analogy. The logic of the concrete, he says, is the mental equivalent of *bricolage* – intellectual D.I.Y.

Lévi-Strauss's notion of *bricolage* has many different applications for all of those, from anthropologists to literary critics and philosophers, who have recognized themselves in his portrait of the *bricoleur* and drawn their own lessons from it.

Lévi-Strauss contrasts the work of the *bricoleur* to that of the engineer, and uses this opposition to characterize the two modes of understanding which underlie, respectively, primitive science and modern science.

At the same time, he also applies his concept of *bricolage* to myth, thus opening up the whole question of its specific relevance to an understanding of the processes of artistic creation.

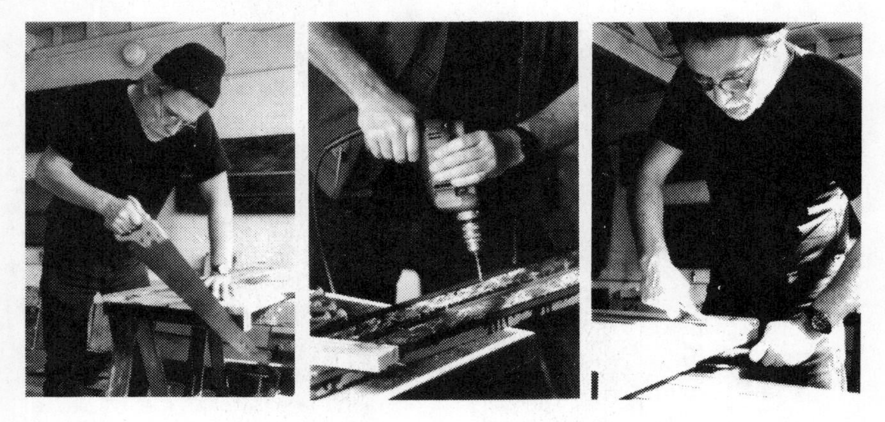

Throughout my description of the BRICOLEUR, the figure of the artist is never far away.

This is how the *bricoleur* works.

Unlike the engineer who creates specialized tools and materials for each new project that he embarks upon, the *bricoleur* works with materials that are always second hand.

MY OBJECTS ARE MADE OUT OF THE DEBRIS AND RESIDUE OF OTHER CREATIONS THAT I COLLECT AND REASSEMBLE.

In as much as he must make do with whatever is at hand, an element of chance always enters into the work of the *bricoleur*.

Lévi-Strauss draws two analogies with myth. First, considered in its genesis, myth, like *bricolage*, is an assembly of disparate elements: it creates structures (i.e. narratives) out of events.

Second, myths are always constructed out of the disarticulated elements of the social discourses of the past. In this too they resemble *bricolage*.

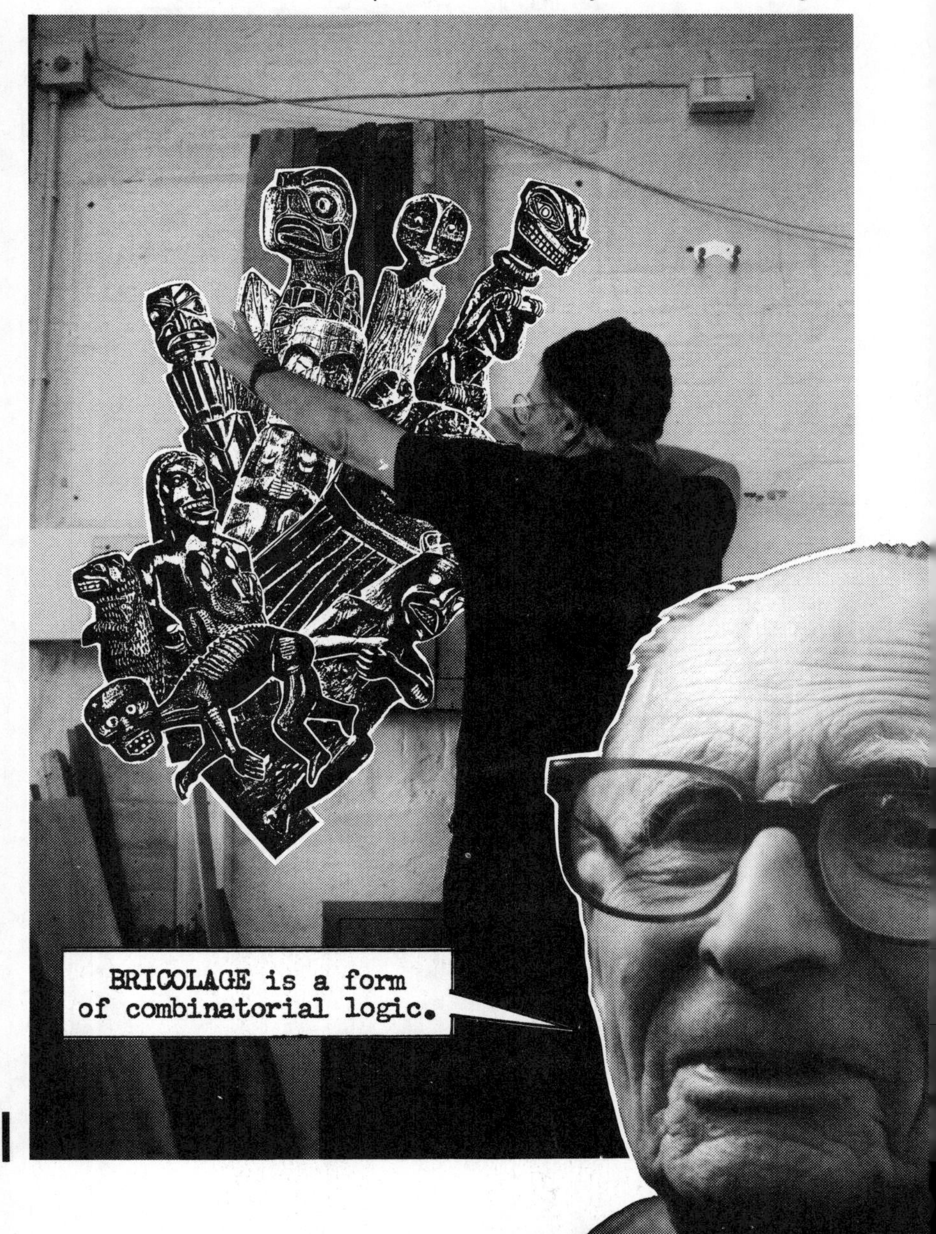
BRICOLAGE is a form of combinatorial logic.

The *bricoleur* is in possession of a stock of objects (a "treasure"). These possess "meaning" in as much as they are bound together by a set of possible relationships, one of which is concretized by the *bricoleur*'s choice.

Thus, a block of oak may be used as a wedge to fix something in place, or, alternatively, as a plinth for an art object to stand on.

IN THE FIRST CASE IT WOULD CONSTITUTE AN EXPANSE.
IN THE SECOND, IT WOULD BECOME TEXTURE, AND THE GRAIN AND POLISH OF THE WOOD WOULD BE BROUGHT OUT.

WORKING WITH SIGNS

In primitive science, the object that the scientist-*bricoleur* deconstructs and reassembles like an old clock is nature itself. The logic of the concrete proceeds by combining and opposing in various ways elements of perception selected from nature. Primitive science is a form of *bricolage* in which the primary materials used are **percepts**, or rather, to be more precise, percepts promoted to the rank of signs.

PERCEPTS ARE THE IMAGES IN OUR MINDS OF THE OBJECTS WE PERCEIVE. THESE BECOME SIGNS WHEN THEY ARE USED IN THE CONSTRUCTION OF SYMBOLIC SYSTEMS.

Lévi-Strauss says that while the engineer works with concepts, the *bricoleur* – in his many guises – works with signs. Concepts are "transparent to reality" – i.e. they interpose no material body between the idea and the world – whereas signs are concrete objects that already bear the mark of the process of human invention. We can understand this in Saussurian linguistic terms.

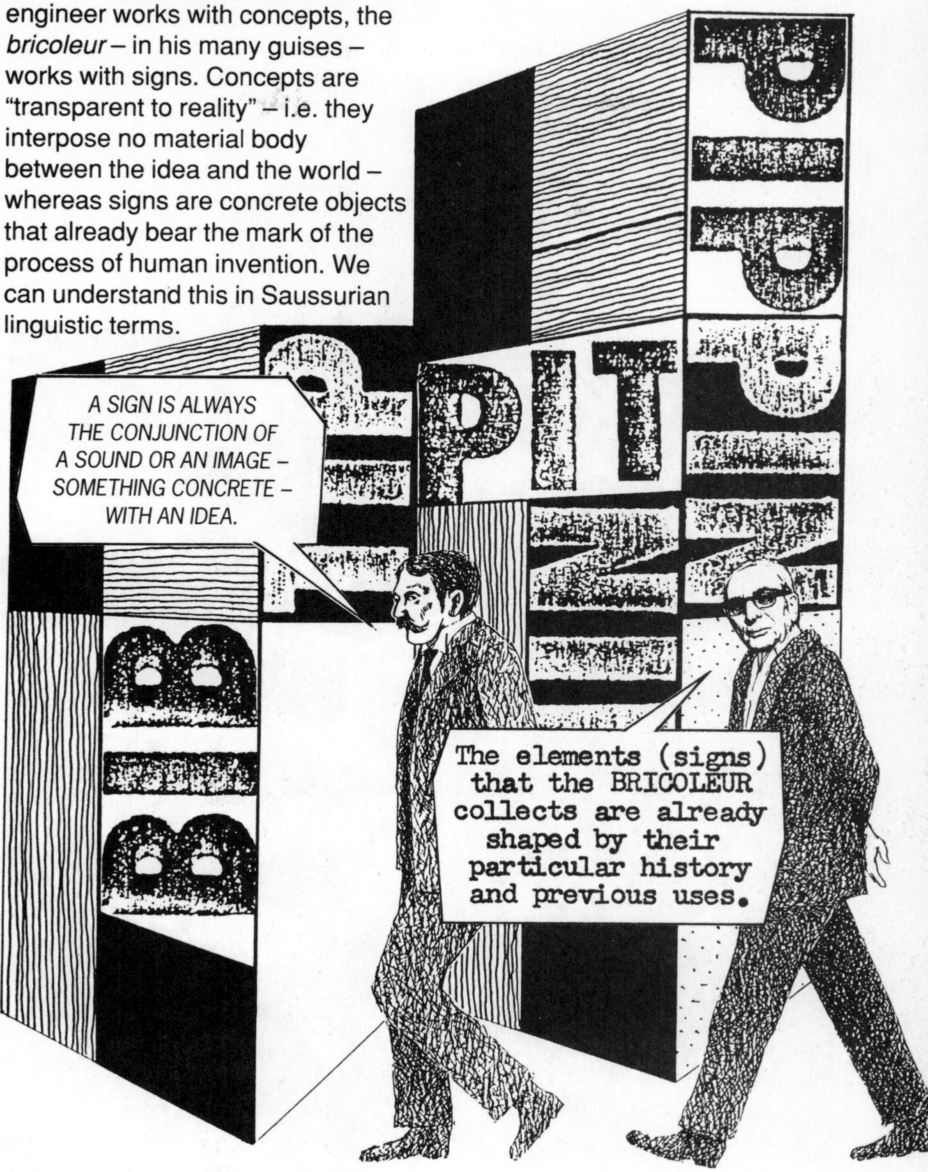

A SIGN IS ALWAYS THE CONJUNCTION OF A SOUND OR AN IMAGE – SOMETHING CONCRETE – WITH AN IDEA.

The elements (signs) that the BRICOLEUR collects are already shaped by their particular history and previous uses.

They contain, embedded in them, fragments of their past meaning (usage) with which the *bricoleur* is forced to compose. Hence the possibilities open to the *bricoleur* are always limited and in a sense predetermined.

The engineer or the modern scientist is constantly expanding the boundaries of the set within which he works. His efforts always aim to go beyond what is already known and possible. With structures (his theories and hypotheses) he produces events in the form of discoveries and inventions.

On the other hand, the *bricoleur* collects and rearranges the elements of previously transmitted "messages" which he seeks to order in new ways. But he does not change the nature of the objects that he dismantles, simply their internal organization.

What then is the point of his work? The *bricoleur* seeks to find new combinatorial variations in his quest for meaning. The work of the *bricoleur* is, as Lévi-Strauss puts it, *une protestation contre le non-sens* – a protest against meaninglessness.

The BRICOLEUR always reveals something about himself through the objects that he creates. Every choice that he makes says something about his own life and character.

LÉVI-STRAUSS AND THE PRAGUE CONNECTION

Saussure's principles of structural linguistics were taken up and developed by the highly influential Prague Linguistic Circle whose theories were to be of great importance to the structuralists. Among the founding members of the Prague Circle was **Roman Jakobson** (1896–1982). Born in Moscow, Jakobson moved as a young man to Czechoslovakia where he led much of the work of the Prague Circle.

When German troops invaded Czechoslovakia in 1939, Jakobson fled and finally left Europe for America. He arrived in New York in 1941. There he met Lévi-Strauss and their lifelong friendship began. Both taught at the Ecole Libre des Hautes Etudes in New York and in 1942 they began to attend each other's lectures.

What was so important about the exchange of ideas that took place between these two men?

ROMAN JAKOBSON
I decided to incorporate the lessons of structural linguistics into anthropology.
IN DOING THIS, HE OPENED THE WAY TO USING LINGUISTIC METHODS AND THEORIES IN OTHER FIELDS, IN PARTICULAR THE SOCIAL SCIENCES.
BUT THESE METHODS WERE ALSO FOUND TO BE APPLICABLE TO LITERARY CRITICISM . . .
. . . AND TO PSYCHOANALYSIS.
JACQUES LACAN
ROLAND BARTHES

Lévi-Strauss indicated for a whole generation of thinkers how to use linguistics in their research. Structural linguistics stressed the fact that languages are relational structures or systems. As John Lyons, Professor of Linguistics at the University of Edinburgh, puts it: "Linguistic units are but points in a system, or network, of relations; they are the terminals of these relations, and they have no prior and independent existence."

From this, Lévi-Strauss derives the golden rule of structural anthropology: that the interrelations between elements are always more important than the elements in themselves – the very essence of the structuralist creed.

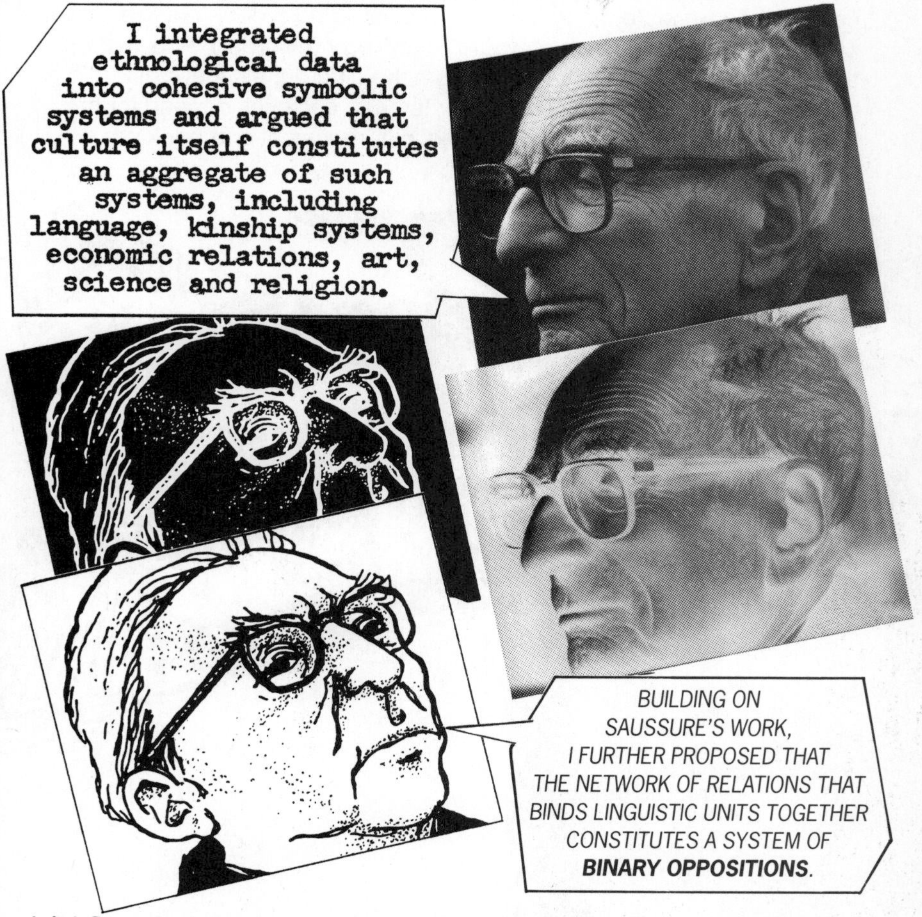

I integrated ethnological data into cohesive symbolic systems and argued that culture itself constitutes an aggregate of such systems, including language, kinship systems, economic relations, art, science and religion.
BUILDING ON SAUSSURE'S WORK, I FURTHER PROPOSED THAT THE NETWORK OF RELATIONS THAT BINDS LINGUISTIC UNITS TOGETHER CONSTITUTES A SYSTEM OF **BINARY OPPOSITIONS**.

Lévi-Strauss, following Jakobson, revealed the importance of binary oppositions and other structuring dichotomies in the symbolic systems created by man. This has become one of the hallmarks of Lévi-Strauss's structural method.

HOT AND COLD SOCIETIES

Lévi-Strauss chose to name the penultimate chapter of *The Savage Mind,* "Time Regained", the title of the last volume of the novel *A la Recherche du temps perdu* by **Marcel Proust** (1871–1922). The relationship of primitive cultures to time (history) is introduced in this way.

There are two kinds of societies, says Lévi-Strauss: "hot" and "cold". The former – the "hot" model on which Western societies are built – may be compared to thermodynamic machines (steam engines). They are capable of carrying out a lot of work – i.e. creating order – but like steam engines also produce a lot of waste or **entropy** (disorder). And, just as steam engines derive their energy from the differentials that exist between their hot and cold components, "hot" societies depend for their functioning on the existence of internal differences of another kind: **social hierarchies**.

WRITING AND SOCIAL HIERARCHIES

The emergence of these hierarchies, Lévi-Strauss argues, is intimately related to the invention of **writing**, an instrument of power that came to be used by one class for controlling another. The first uses of writing seem to have been the making of laws and rules, the drawing up of contracts, the making of inventories.

These are all modes whereby one section of society imposes its power over another.

A WRITING LESSON

A story told in *Tristes tropiques* (1955), in a chapter entitled "The Writing Lesson", tells how the introduction of writing into a society where it had previously not existed brings in its wake social manipulation and division. Observing Lévi-Strauss taking notes in the jungle, the chief of the tribe perceived the power and status which this act conferred upon the anthropologist in the eyes of his fellow tribesmen.

He took up pen and paper himself and set out to imitate the magical act.

Since he could not write, all he could do was draw undulating lines on a sheet of paper, but this proved to be equally effective in giving him even greater standing among his fellow tribesmen.

Jacques Derrida (b. 1930), the controversial exponent of deconstruction, takes up this anecdote in what has become a seminal post-structuralist text, *Of Grammatology* (1967).

I READ LÉVI-STRAUSS'S STORY AS THE ANTHROPOLOGIST'S NOSTALGIC VALUING OF SPEECH (PRESENCE) OVER WRITING – SOMETHING WHICH I SEE AS A FEATURE OF MUCH OF WESTERN THOUGHT.

For Derrida, writing is **always already** present in culture.

HOW COLD SOCIETIES RESIST CHANGE

One definition of "cold" societies is that they are societies without writing. They are compared by Lévi-Strauss to clocks, which are mechanisms that go on functioning for a long time using the same small energetic charge that set them in motion. Their aim is to maintain themselves in a state of equilibrium, minimizing "friction". In this respect, "cold" societies are more egalitarian (as well as ecological) than their thermodynamic big brothers.

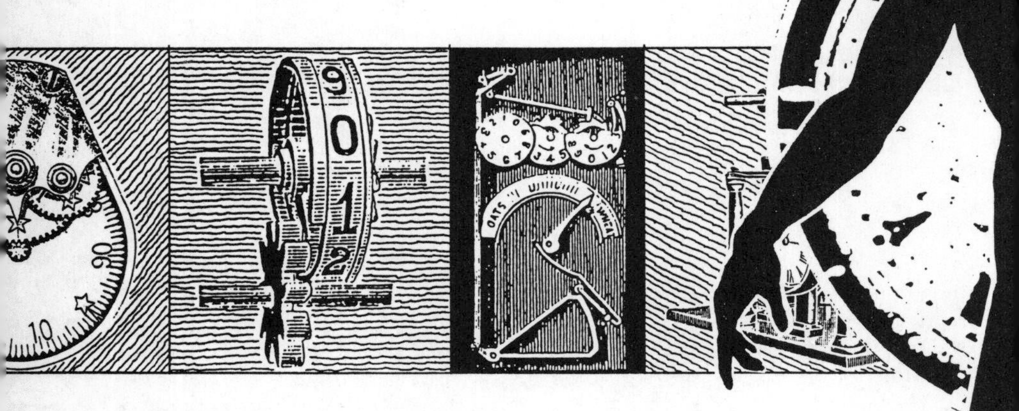

They are societies that seek to "cancel out", as much as possible, the effects of history. Their aim is to resist change.

How do "cold" societies resist change? By assigning to their institutions, socio-political practices and systems of representation a **homeostatic** (self-regulating) function. This comes out in their use of rituals and classificatory systems.

Lévi-Strauss describes a funerary rite among the Fox Indians. It involves playing a game that symbolically opposes the living and the dead.

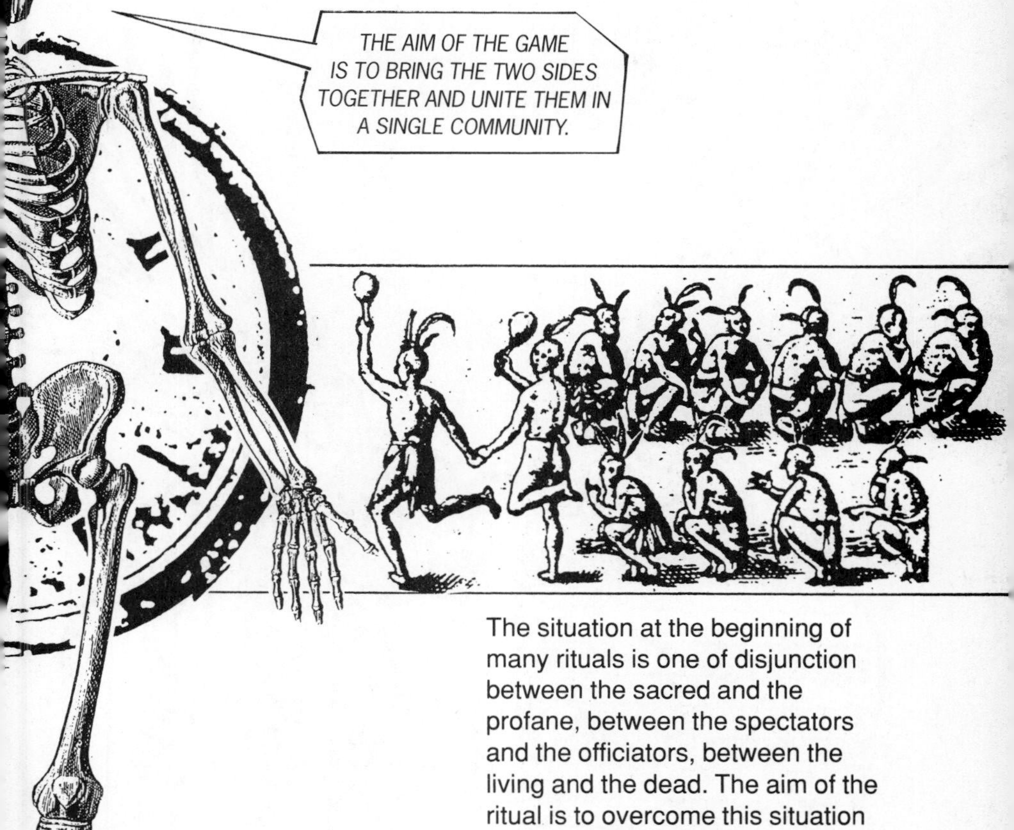

THE AIM OF THE GAME IS TO BRING THE TWO SIDES TOGETHER AND UNITE THEM IN A SINGLE COMMUNITY.

The situation at the beginning of many rituals is one of disjunction between the sacred and the profane, between the spectators and the officiators, between the living and the dead. The aim of the ritual is to overcome this situation and bring about a union of these two classes of individuals.

GAMES, RITUALS AND CLASSIFICATIONS

Rituals are the opposite of games. Games – an activity characteristic of "hot" societies – use structures (the rules of the game) to produce events (victories or defeats). They are fundamentally **disjunctive**, as their aim is to separate the winner from the loser. Rituals are **conjunctive** – their aim is to bring together.

The Gahuku-Gama from New Guinea were taught to play football. But the tournaments they devised have a unique twist to them.

WE PLAY AS MANY GAMES AS ARE NECESSARY FOR THE OPPOSING TEAMS TO ARRIVE AT AN EQUAL SCORE.

They assigned to the game the exact function of a ritual.

Classificatory systems (the conceptual tools by means of which primitive cultures order their world) fulfil a similar function to rituals. They too serve the purpose of integrating events (the contingent) into structures (a code). To borrow an expression Lévi-Strauss uses to describe music: "they are machines for the suppression of time".

Totemic classifications, which use the names of animal or plant species to create nomenclatures for social groups, are designed to adapt constantly to demographic changes, such as a sudden rise or fall in a population level.

THESE CHANGES DO NOT SUBSTANTIALLY ALTER THE NATURE OF THE TOTEMIC SYSTEM, BUT BRING ABOUT A REORGANIZATION OF ITS INTERNAL STRUCTURE.

Lévi-Strauss postulates a tribe made up of three clans named respectively after the bear, the eagle and the turtle, a nomenclature corresponding to a three-way opposition between earth, sky and water. Should the clan of the bear come to die out, and the clan of the turtle increase in numbers to a point where it divides into two (yellow turtle and grey turtle), the underlying system reorganizes itself to fit the new situation.

The three-way opposition gives way to a four-term opposition made up of two binary oppositions.

sky and water
day and night

Each is associated with one type of turtle.

Classificatory systems of this kind are the regulatory mechanisms that keep primitive cultures "cool".

Lévi-Strauss compares totemic classifications to a palace carried away by a river. It is first of all dismembered but only to be continually rearranged in accordance with the water's ebb and flow and the obstacles it encounters on its way.

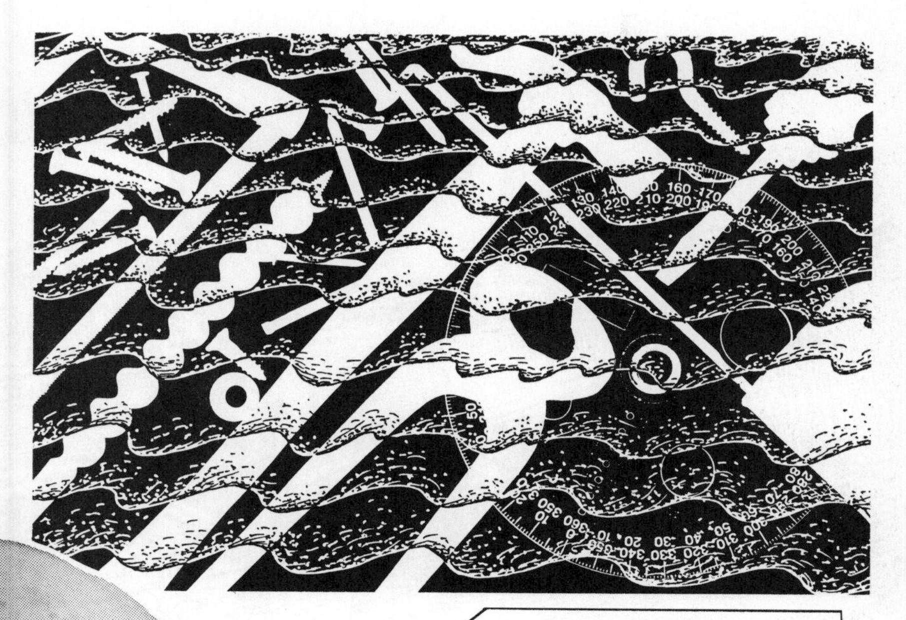

I am not saying that primitive societies actually exist outside history, or in some different temporal dimension. Like any other society, they have a past that has played its part in shaping their present state.

He is interested in "history" as a cultural category, and how different cultures situate themselves in relationship to this category.

HISTORY AS LINEAR TIME: HOT SOCIETIES

What matters is the different ways in which "hot" and "cold" societies conceptualize their relationship to time – how they envisage their own being-in-time. For, as Lévi-Strauss points out, the image that a society has of itself is an essential part of its own reality.

The image of time makes the essential difference between "hot" and "cold" societies.

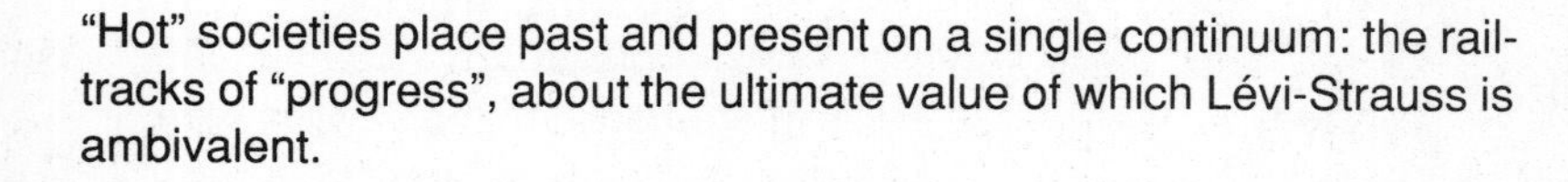

"Hot" societies place past and present on a single continuum: the rail-tracks of "progress", about the ultimate value of which Lévi-Strauss is ambivalent.

Time is represented as a cumulative sequence, each moment stemming from the previous one and announcing the next.

Such a representation of time is inseparable from the value "hot" societies place on change (progress). "Hot" societies, says Lévi-Strauss, "internalize the notion of historical time as the motor of their development."

History is a category inherent in certain societies, a way in which hierarchical ("hot") societies apprehend their own being, and not an environment in which all human groups are situated in the same way.

History is a human construct, a cultural invention.

TIME AS A CIRCLE: COLD SOCIETIES

In contrast, “cold” (traditional) societies conceive of the present as at once emerging from the past *and as parallel to it*. Let’s take the example of Amerindian cultures.

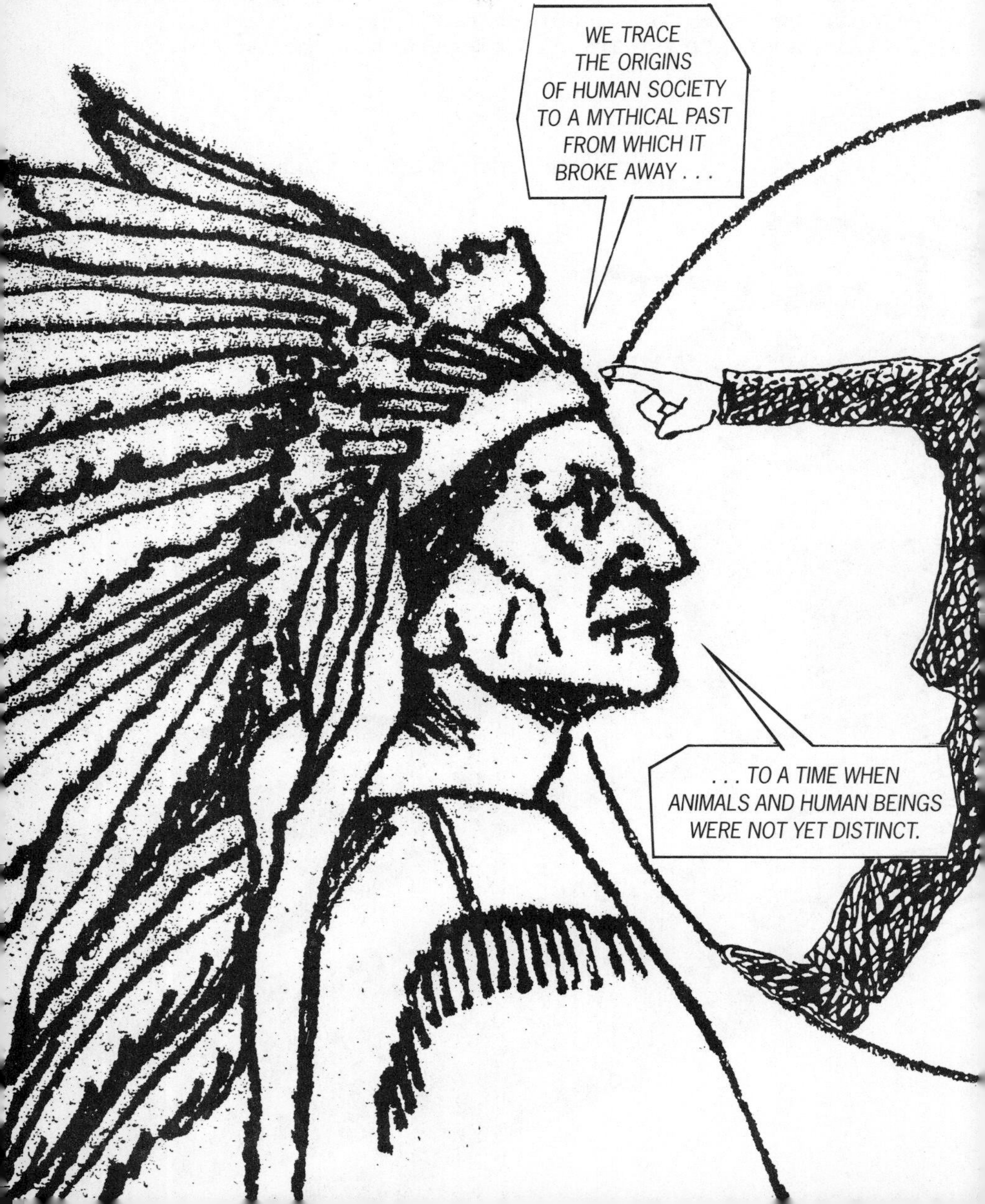

WE TRACE THE ORIGINS OF HUMAN SOCIETY TO A MYTHICAL PAST FROM WHICH IT BROKE AWAY . . .
. . . TO A TIME WHEN ANIMALS AND HUMAN BEINGS WERE NOT YET DISTINCT.

This mythical past continues to exist, in a kind of a-temporal mode, embodied in nature. And human society is interpreted as a projection of this order perceived in nature.

In "cold" societies there is indeed, says Lévi-Strauss, a "before" and an "after", but their function is to reflect one another.

Time is inscribed in a circle.

LÉVI-STRAUSSIAN AESTHETICS

The understanding of art has always been of great importance to Lévi-Strauss.

FOR THE ANTHROPOLOGIST, THE WORKS OF ART PRODUCED BY PRIMITIVE POPULATIONS ARE INVALUABLE DOCUMENTS.
THEY PROVIDE VITAL INFORMATION ABOUT A SOCIETY'S BELIEFS AND SOCIAL ORGANIZATION.
IN THIS RESPECT, THEY ARE AN IMPORTANT TOOL OF ANTHROPOLOGICAL UNDERSTANDING.
But these same works of art can also be the source of profound aesthetic emotion and therefore of aesthetic reflection.

For Lévi-Strauss, primitive art has always been both of these things – document and aesthetic object.

Throughout his studies of the works of art of primitive cultures – whether the masks and costumes of the Indians of British Columbia or the myths of the Indians of the Brazilian rain forests – Lévi-Strauss has developed a concept of aesthetics that derives its freshness from its intimate relationship with primitive art whose lessons he has sought to decrypt.

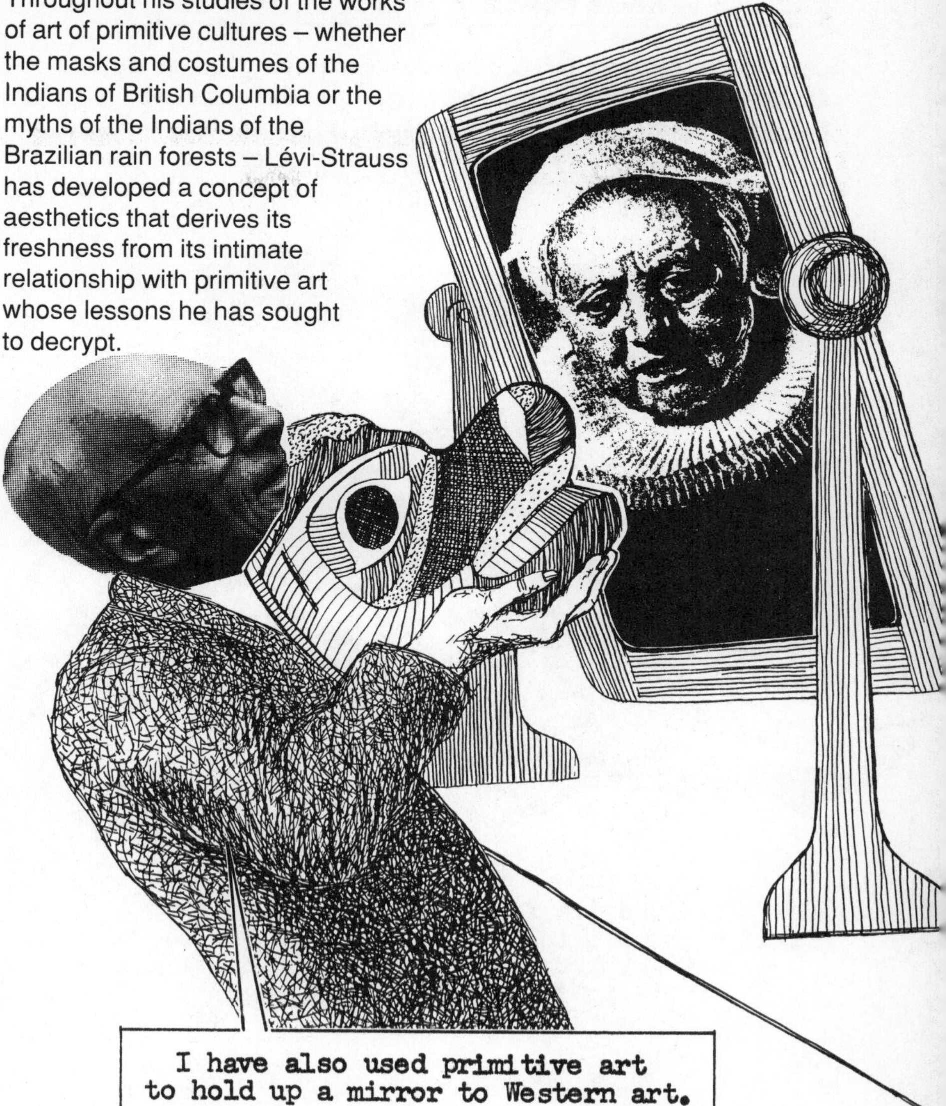

I have also used primitive art to hold up a mirror to Western art.

"My interest in myths stems from a deep emotion which I cannot explain. What is a beautiful object? What does aesthetic emotion consist of? Maybe, in the end, without being fully aware of it, this is what I have been trying to understand through my study of myths?" [CL-S]

SIGNS VERSUS MIMESIS

Lévi-Strauss opposes two conceptions of the work of art: as a **system of signs** and as **mimetic representation**. These designate two broad paths open to the artist. The first, he says, is characteristic of the art of primitive cultures, the second of Western art in its classical forms.

The distinctive feature of primitive art is that it does not aim to REPRESENT things (in the way that a photograph does) but rather to SIGNIFY them, in the manner of language.

Its aim is not imitation, or in Greek, *mimesis* – one of the principal goals assigned to Western art ever since Plato and Aristotle – but to construct a system of signs. This contrasts with classical Western art whose primary objective is to create the illusion of the object represented – a "facsimile", says Lévi-Strauss.

The primitive artist is limited by the material constraints which are his own. He does not have the tools or materials with which to create faithful representations of things.

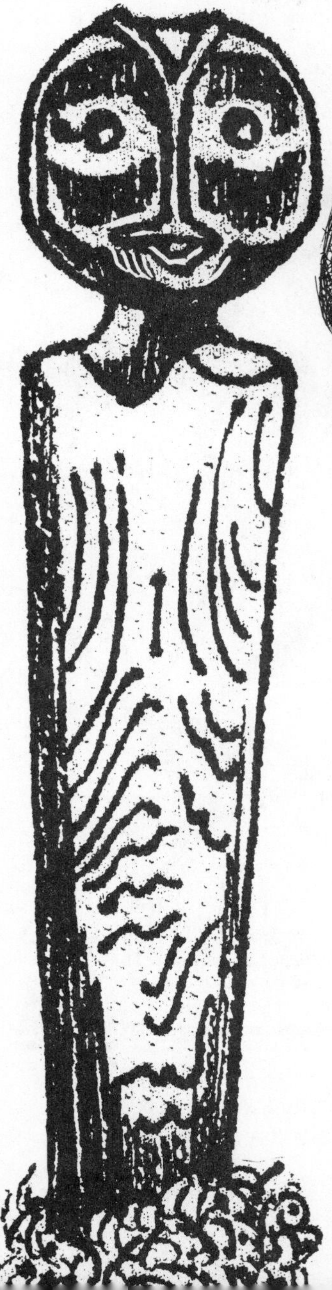

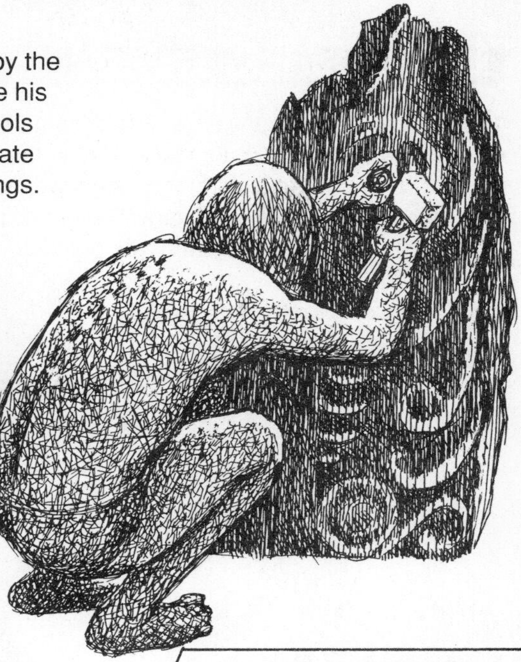

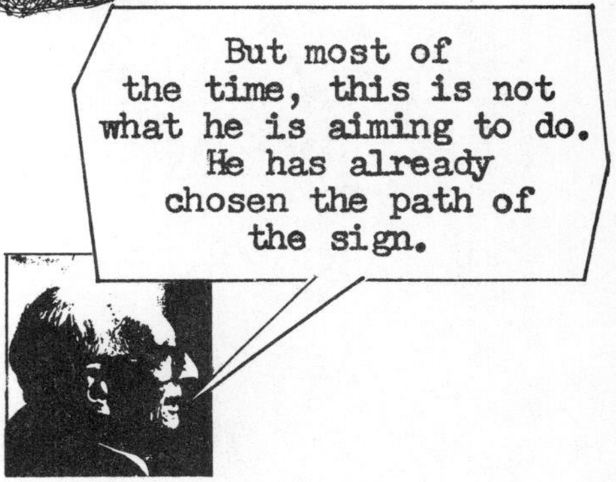

But most of the time, this is not what he is aiming to do. He has already chosen the path of the sign.

This has got to do with the particular relationship that exists in primitive cultures between art and magical or religious beliefs. The world of primitive cultures is one steeped in the supernatural and therefore, by definition, it escapes representation. Its duplicate image ("facsimile") cannot be given by the artist. For the primitive artist, "the model always exceeds its image".

PRIMITIVISM IN WESTERN ART

This conception of the work of art as a sign system (as opposed to a mimetic representation) is characteristic not only of primitive cultures but of a form of "primitivism" that is an intermittently recurring feature of Western art. The style of early Greek sculpture which flourished until the 5th century B.C. is an art of the signifier . . .

. . . whereas the style that replaced it – typified by the famous "Discobolus" of **Myron** (c. 450 B.C.) – was more "naturalistic", i.e. representational.

This was also the case with Italian painting until the *quattrocento* (the 1400s), that is, up to and including the Siennese school.

DUCCIO (1260-1319)
MANTEGNA (1431-1506)

Lévi-Strauss relates the high value attached by Western art since the Renaissance to figuration, to a desire to *possess* the object – particularly the beautiful object – by the means of its effigy.

MODERNIST ART

Modern art since Cubism is in many ways a form of "primitivist" art in the Lévi-Straussian sense – it is an art of the signifier, one that is conceptual rather than perceptual.

Lévi-Strauss, however, contrary to what one might expect, considers Cubism to have been a failed aesthetic revolution and the abstract movement that emerged out of it a dead-end. He explains his attitude to Cubism in the following way.

Cubism aspired to become a new aesthetic LANGUAGE, but all languages, by definition, exist in and through the group.

For socio-economic reasons that are beyond the artist's control, the processes of production and consumption of works of art in Western societies have become divorced from the group as a whole ("individualized"). Therefore, Cubism, although it aspires to achieve a new aesthetic language, is no more than an "idiolect" (language as used by an individual person).

For Lévi-Strauss, the "art of the signifier" has to arise naturally out of the group's heritage – its culture – and cannot be imposed from outside by an individual imitating this style of art for effect.

The idea that the work of art is an object **analogous** to language is central to Lévi-Strauss's aesthetic thought.

HENDRIK NICOLAAS WERKMAN (1882-1945)
This is not to say that art IS a language, but that it RESEMBLES one.

He is careful not to assimilate the work of art to language and reduce it to a mere system of communication. To do so would be to remove its specifically aesthetic value.

THE RELATION OF ART TO LANGUAGE

Like language, the work of art is a system of signs, but unlike language, in art the relationship between signifier and signified is not **arbitrary**.

Arbitrariness is one of the so-called "design features" of human languages. What linguists mean by the "arbitrariness" of language is that the relationship that links any given linguistic sign – such as the word "tree" – to the thing it signifies (its referent) is purely a matter of convention. There is no inherent reason why one sign should be used instead of any other.

What an English speaker designates with the phonemes: /T/ /R/ /E/ /E/...
. . . A FRENCH SPEAKER DESIGNATES WITH THE PHONEMES: /A/ /R/ /B/ /R/ /E/.

The particularity of the work of art, construed as a system of signs, is that of a deep **homology** between the structure of the signifier and that of the signified. It is not a system of arbitrary signs, but one in which there continues to exist a **perceptible** link between the sign and what it denotes – and thus structures common to both are brought to light.

THE ART OF MASKS

One day in 1941, Lévi-Strauss, at the time living in exile in New York, made a trip to the American Museum of Natural History. There he discovered for the first time, in a kind of aesthetic revelation, the art of the Northwest coast Indians. (The moment is beautifully described in the opening section of his book, *The Way of the Masks*, 1975.)

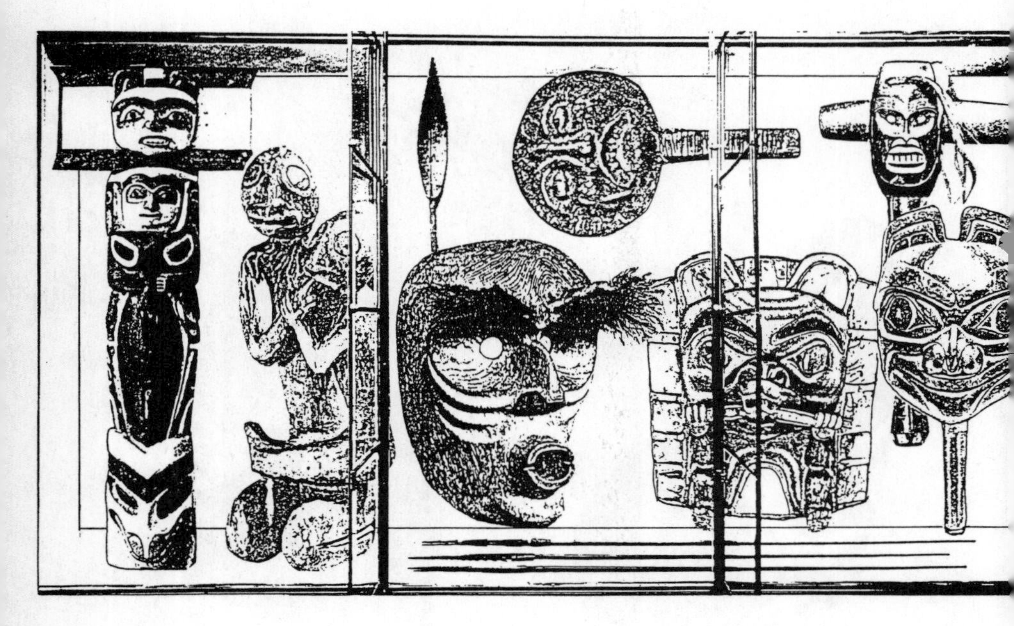

These Indians occupy a territory that stretches the length of the Pacific coast from British Columbia to Alaska. A great diversity of art forms were invented by them. The Chilkat made magnificent embroidered capes dyed in yellow, black and blue. The Tlingit developed a subtle statuary. But it was their masks that Lévi-Strauss found to be the most striking and fascinating.

The Way of the Masks tries to understand the provenance of some of the more enigmatic formal features of the masks. Lévi-Strauss focused in particular on three types of masks, the **Xwé Xwé**, the **Swaihwé** and the **Dzonokwa** that are the property of a small group of neighbouring populations.

He came to understand that these masks had not been created independently by each tribal group but formed part of an overarching system of transformations.

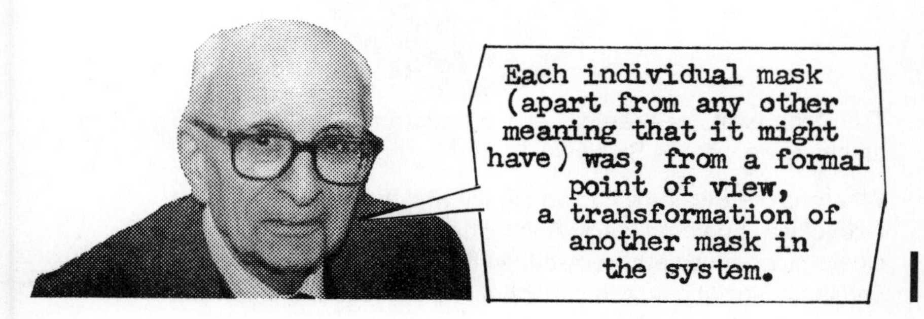
Each individual mask (apart from any other meaning that it might have) was, from a formal point of view, a transformation of another mask in the system.

A SYSTEM OF LINKS

Each type of mask was defined by a set of distinctive features (colours, shapes, symbolic associations) which were constitutive of its particular style and at once correlated and opposed to the features of other masks.

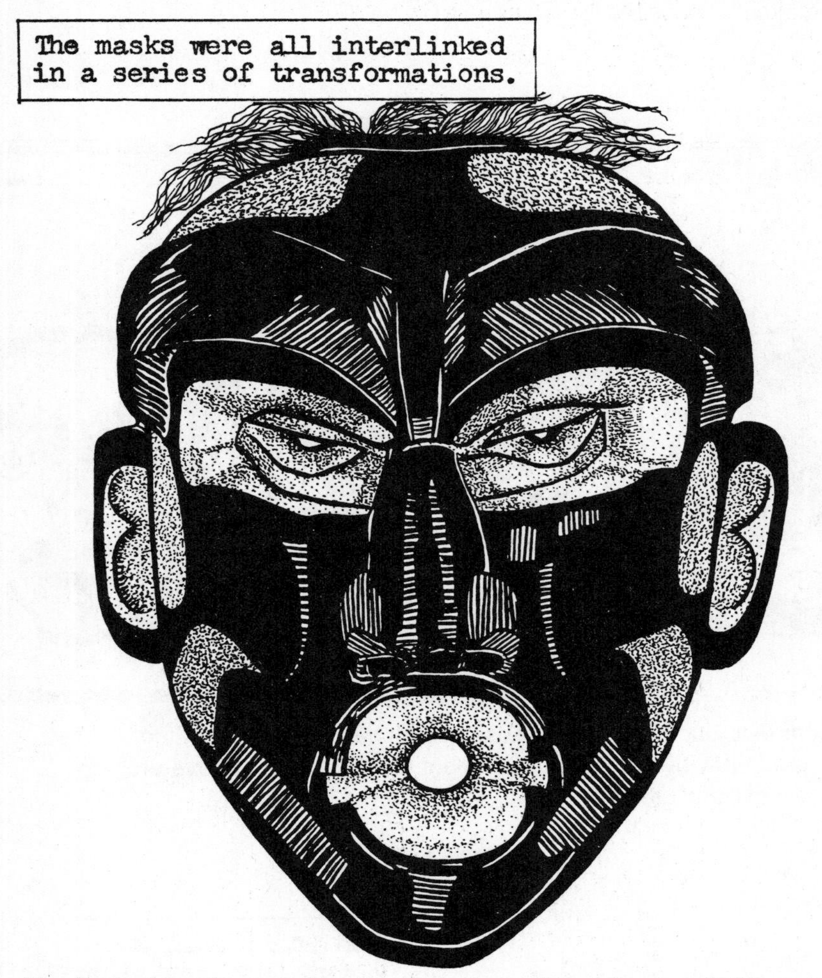
The masks were all interlinked in a series of transformations.

The Dzonokwa, for example, is a logical transformation – or in this case an inversion – of the Swaihwé.

Whereas the Swaihwé has an affinity with the colour white, the Dzonokwa is painted black. Animal hair, signifying a beard, and a fur cloak (of a dark colour) replace, on the Dzonokwa, the feather crown and the associations with birds that characterize the Swaihwé.

The eyes of the Dzonokwa mask are represented as half closed, and instead of protruding like the cylindrical Swaihwé eyes, they are deeply sunken into the sockets. Finally, whereas the lower jaw of the Swaihwé hangs low, exhibiting a tongue through the wide open mouth, the Dzonokwa has a rounded mouth which is positioned in such a way as to make it impossible for a tongue to hang out of it.

Through these formal transformations Lévi-Strauss demonstrated the secret affinity that exists between the Swaihwé and the Dzonokwa.

A mask is chiefly not what it represents but what it transforms, that is, what it chooses NOT to represent.

What does all of this say about what the masks mean?

The masks do not have a single meaning. Rather, like condensed dream images, they are the result of multiple series of semantic associations that relate to their specific cultural contexts.

They are made up of a mosaic of associations that have their origins at once in the myths that are linked to each mask and in the religious, social and economic significances attached to the masks by the social groups that own them.

And these significances are affected by relationships of transformation in exactly the same way that the formal features of the masks are, one type of transformation interacting with and complicating the other.

The Swaihwé mask is owned by the Salish, the Dzonokwa by their neighbours the Kwakiutl. The Dzonokwa is a representation of a legendary female ogre who lives in the depths of a forest.

SHE OCCASIONALLY EMERGES TO ABDUCT KWAKIUTL CHILDREN AND DEVOUR THEM.

The Dzonokwa mask thus represents a disruptive, asocial being who threatens the biological continuity of the social group by abducting its children.

In contrast, the Swaihwé mask is said to represent the founding ancestors of the highest lineages of Salish society, that is, the very guarantors of the biological continuity of the group and of social order. And whereas the Dzonokwa comes from the forest (sometimes the mountains), the myths the Salish tell emphasize the fact that the Swaihwé mask comes either from the sky or from the water.

IT IS SOMETIMES SAID THAT IT WAS FIRST FISHED OUT OF A LAKE. HENCE, THE CONNECTION OCCASIONALLY MADE BETWEEN THE TONGUE OF THE MASK AND THE TAIL OF A FISH.

THE MEANING OF MASKS

Masks have been around from time immemorial and put to many different uses in carnivals, rituals, balls. And of course the Ancient Greeks used them to perform their tragedies.

Societies can be classified into those that possess masks and those that don't.

Why do we wear masks? What meaning do they have for us? Evidently there is no single answer to these questions. However, Lévi-Strauss's anthropological investigations provide us with some keys that we should next consider.

MASKS AND COSMETICS

Lévi-Strauss links masks to cosmetics. Their underlying significance is intimately tied up with the archaic reasons why human populations throughout the world have "painted" their faces, a practice perpetuated today in the use of make-up. The Caduveo used to paint or tattoo their whole bodies with complex patterns of volutes, arabesques and geometrical forms. This practice now survives only among the women.

WE PAINT EACH OTHER'S FACES, ACCORDING TO PRECISE PRE-ESTABLISHED AESTHETIC CANONS.
THOSE WHO ARE NOT PAINTED ARE MERE BEASTS, EXISTING IN A STATE OF NATURE.

The act of painting themselves is first of all an affirmation of their **humanity**, and of the fact that they are **cultural** beings. This is also the significance of masks.

The Caduveo designs are not simply placed ON the face. Their purpose is to split it up and re-create it according to new principles that transform its NATURAL harmonies.

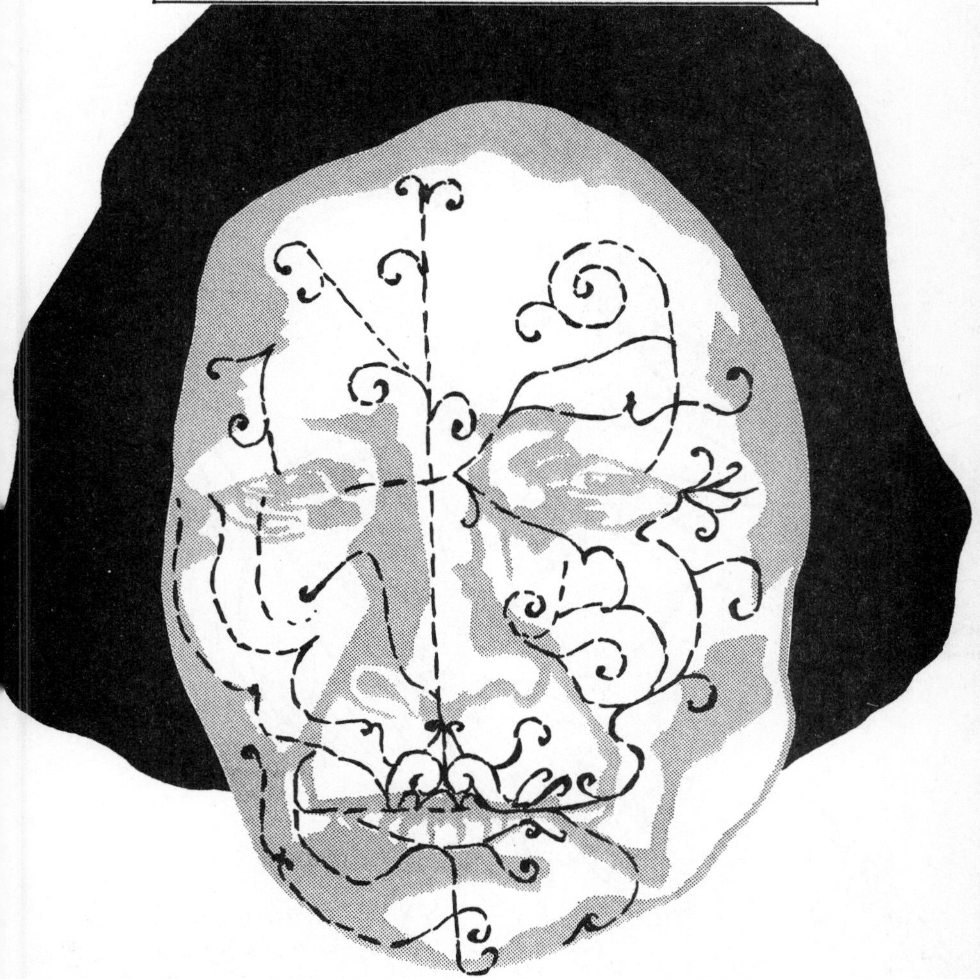

These designs replace natural order with another kind of order created by man.

THE FUNCTIONS OF MASKS

Whatever their aesthetic functions, masks need to be understood in anthropological terms. Every member of a social group is born into a particular clan or family, given a name, inherits a social status. This is an individual's **social costume**.

And it is this "costume" that the mask, with its emblems and insignias indicating rank, social function and role, signifies.

The mask is a universe in miniature, a microcosm in which an individual's place in the social and natural order is reflected.

At the same time, masks fulfil another function: they are the means by which man enters into contact with the world of the supernatural. Lévi-Strauss sees an origin of the mask in the simple gesture of folding one's hair over one's face. The human face is the seat of communication. For communication to occur we need to establish eye contact, speak and be heard.

BY CONCEALING OUR FACES, BY WHATEVER MEANS, THE CIRCUITS OF NORMAL SOCIAL COMMUNICATION ARE INTERRUPTED.

The recognizable individual becomes an anonymous being. He has now shed his social costume, and thus "becomes free to establish contact with other forces, with other worlds, those of love and those of death". The mask re-routes communication away from its social function towards the sacred, the transcendental.

SYMBOLS AND SCALE MODELS

Lévi-Strauss sums up the many meanings of masks in this way.

"Brought to life when it is worn, the mask brings the gods to earth, it reveals their existence, introduces them to the society of men; conversely, by masking himself, man affirms his identity as a social being, expressing and codifying it by means of symbols. The mask is, at once, human and non-human: its very essence is to mediate between society, nature and the supernatural." [CL-S]

Lévi-Strauss has not only written about primitive art. The very first chapter of *The Savage Mind* ends with a long digression that is prompted by the contemplation of a portrait of Queen Elizabeth of Austria by the 16th century French painter **François Clouet** (c. 1520–72).

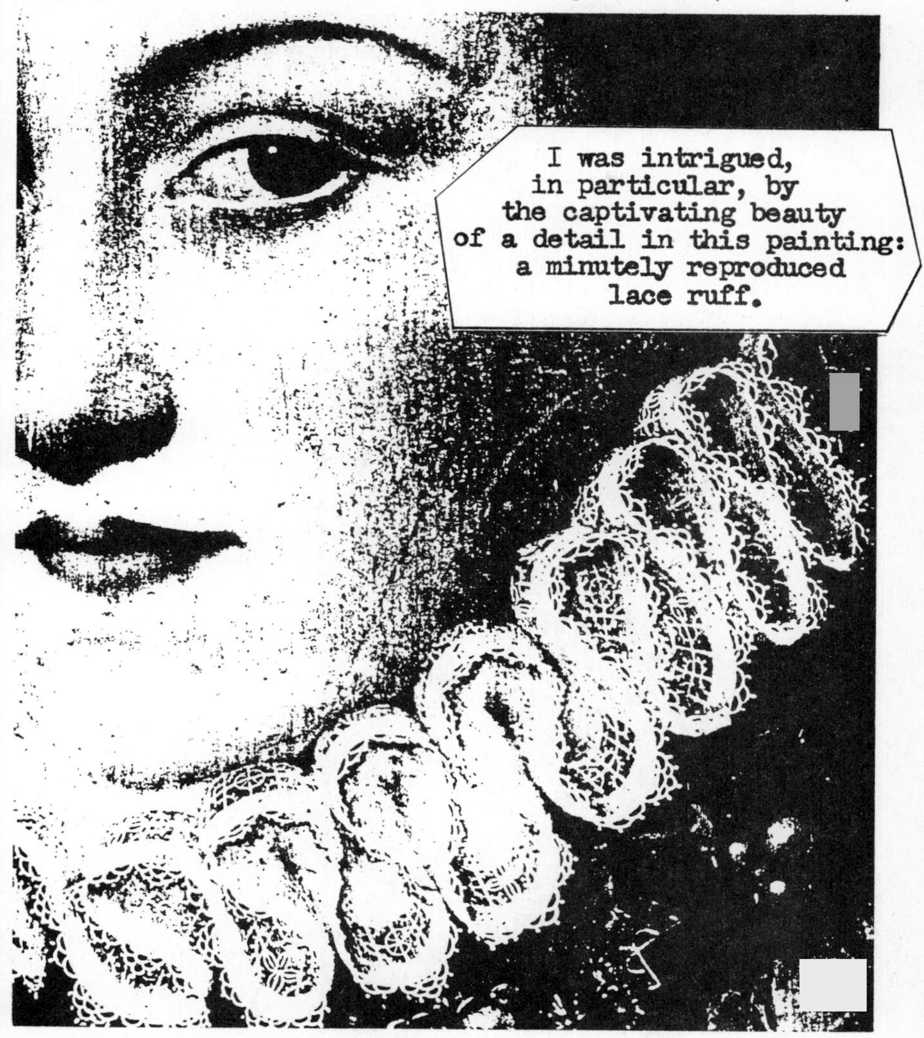
I was intrigued, in particular, by the captivating beauty of a detail in this painting: a minutely reproduced lace ruff.

His ensuing meditations lead him to develop his theory of the *modèle réduit*. All works of art, he argues, partake of the nature of miniatures or scale models (*modèles réduits*), like Japanese gardens, model cars and ships in a bottle.

Let's see in what sense he means this.

REDUCED TO ART

A work of art (Lévi-Strauss is thinking here particularly about representational art) must always forgo one or another of its model's dimensions. It is in this sense that it is "reduced". Painting, for example, must forgo volume, and both painting and sculpture must forgo time.

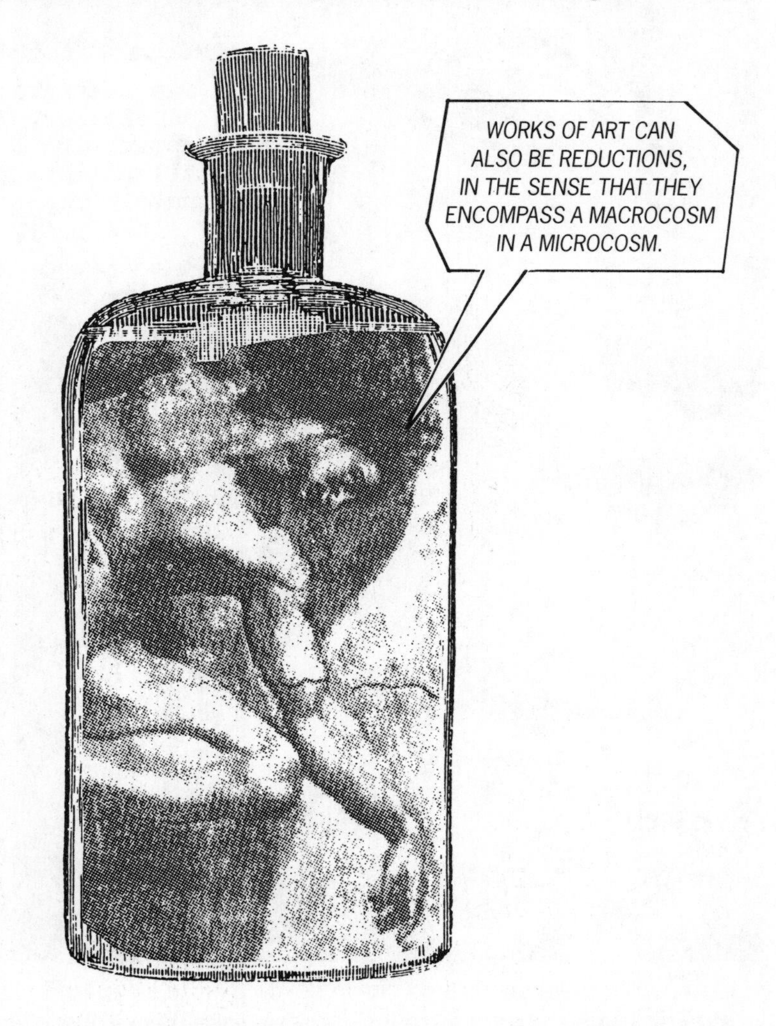
WORKS OF ART CAN ALSO BE REDUCTIONS, IN THE SENSE THAT THEY ENCOMPASS A MACROCOSM IN A MICROCOSM.

This is the case, for example, with Michelangelo's paintings on the ceiling of the Sistine chapel, which despite their great size are nevertheless "miniatures" in relation to the cosmic referent of their subject matter – the Creation.

Works of art are always "simplified" objects, reductions or "scale models" of the realities they reflect. And it is from this fact that they derive their value.

Indeed, the virtue of renouncing certain **sensible** dimensions of an object (as painting does volume for example) is that these are compensated for, in the spectator's mind, by the acquisition of **intelligible** dimensions.

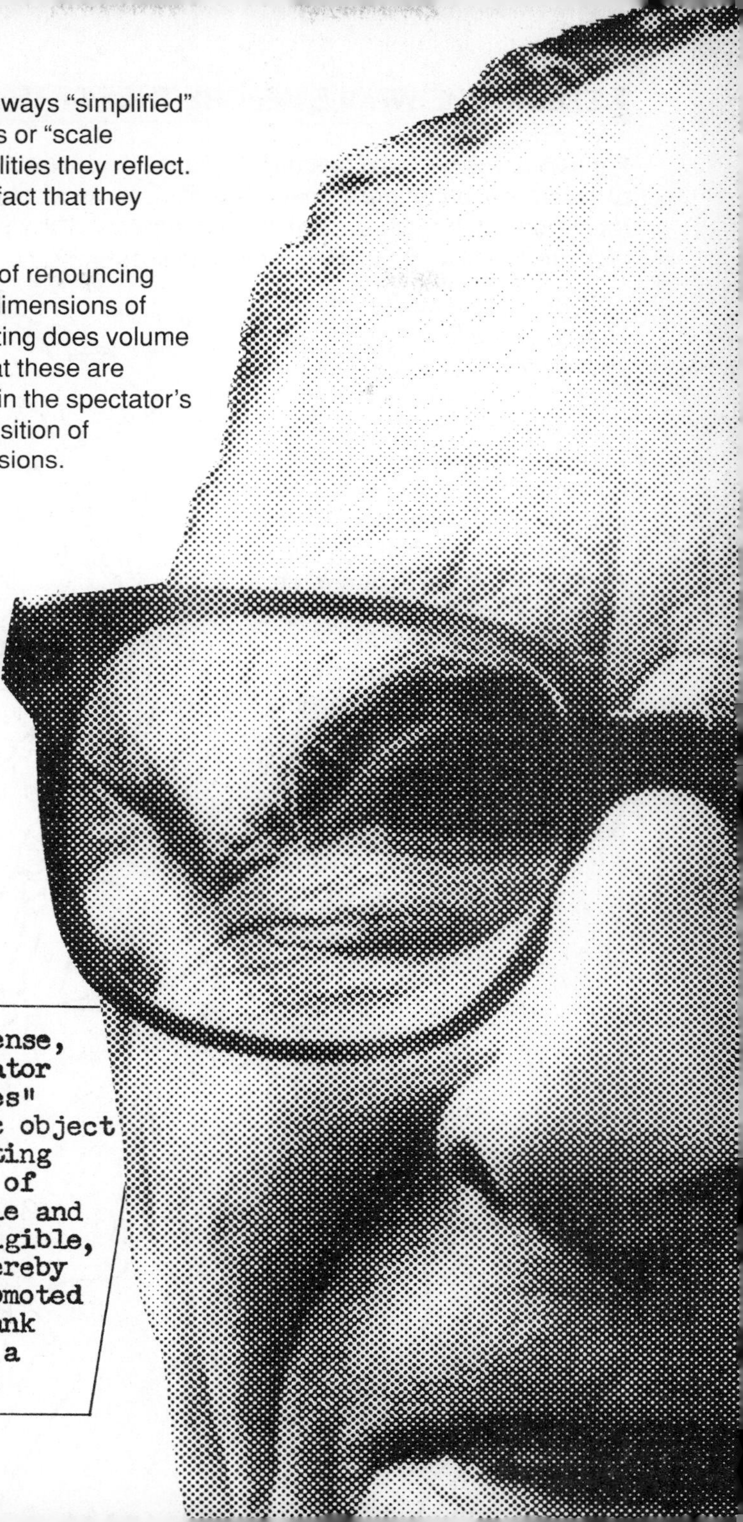

In this sense, the spectator "completes" the aesthetic object by operating a union of the sensible and the intelligible, and is thereby himself promoted to the rank of being a creator.

SEEING THE WHOLE BEFORE THE PARTS

Furthermore, when we contemplate works of art we are aware not only of the work of art before us but of a kind of "table" of other possible realizations of the same work. And each new possibility (transformation), provides us with a new perspective on the work.

Lévi-Strauss introduces another central idea with his theory of the *modèle réduit*. In the way that we apprehend works of art, there occurs what he describes as a *renversement du procès de la connaissance* – an inversion in the chronology of perception. By this he means: the mental procedure whereby we come to "know" an object (recognize it), when that object is a work of art or represented in a work of art, is inverted. In ordinary perception, we reconstruct the whole from the parts. With the work of art, as with the *modèle réduit*, the whole is perceived **before** the parts.

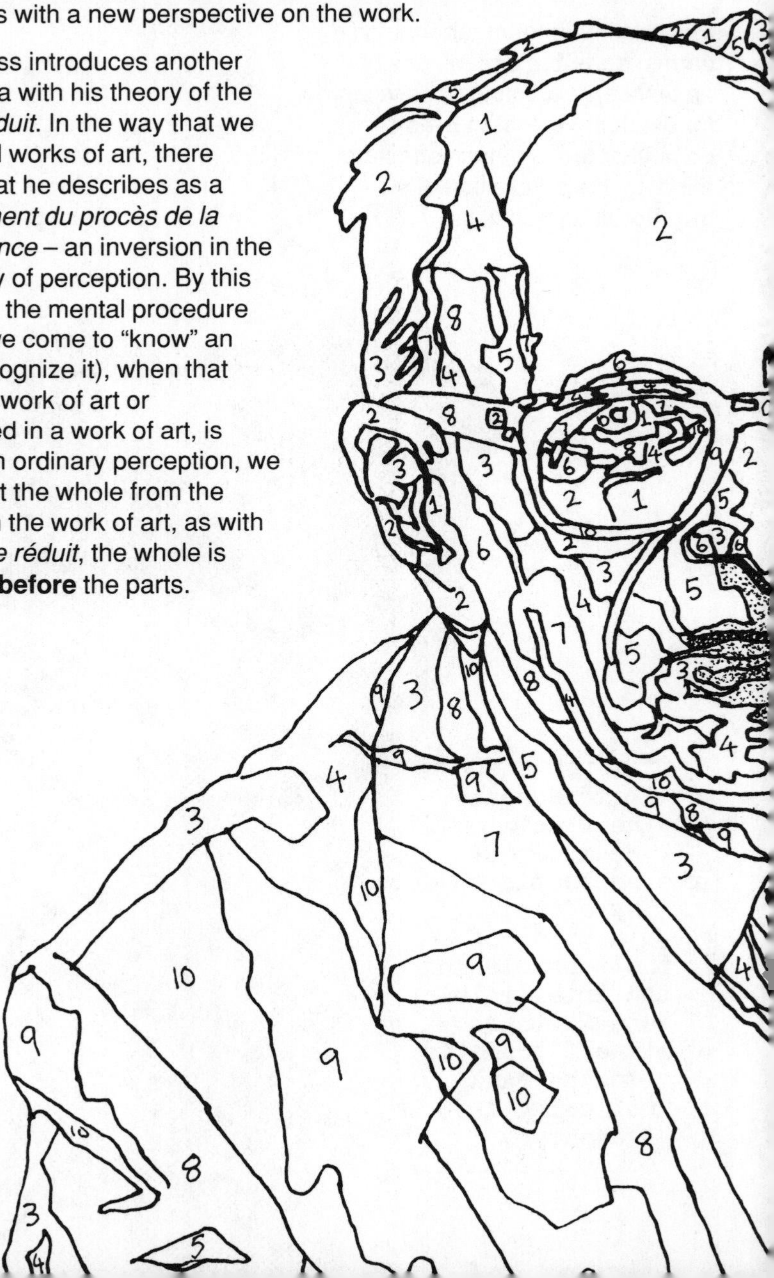

THE ANALOGOUS OBJECT

Lévi-Strauss concedes that this may be no more than an illusion created by the work of art. But it is an illusion, he argues, that gratifies human understanding and sensibility and is at the very root of aesthetic emotion.

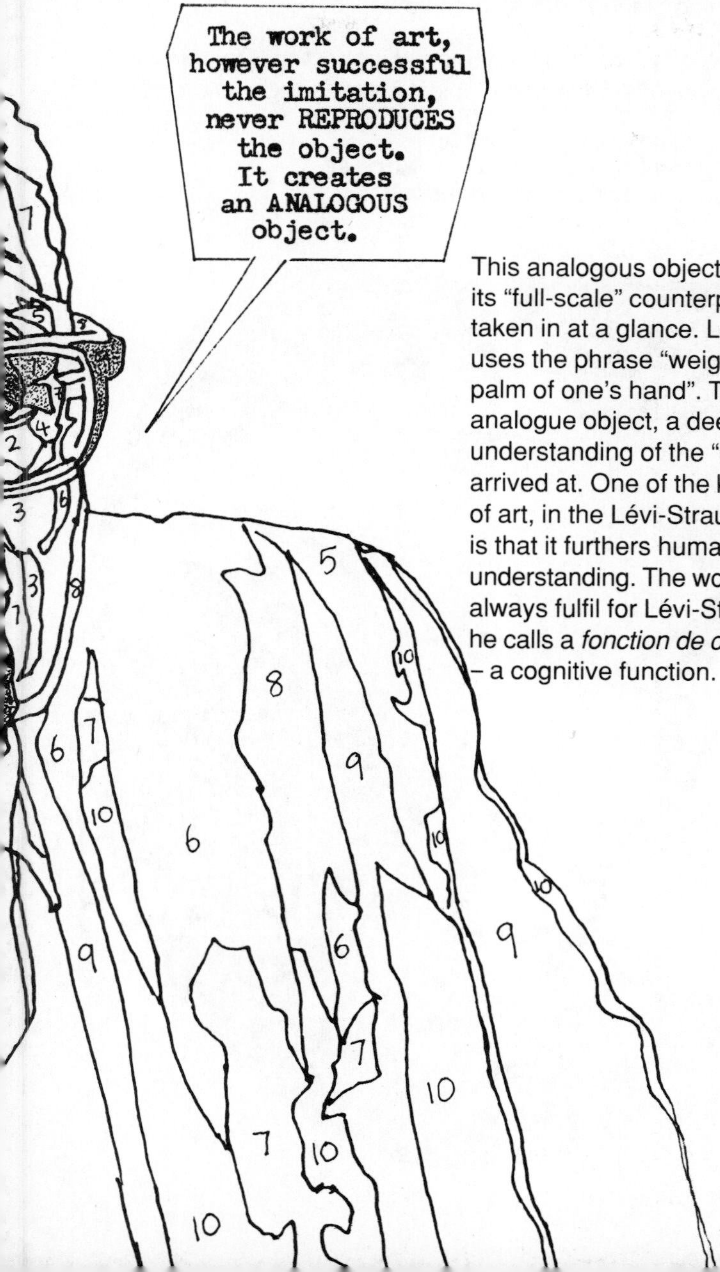

The work of art, however successful the imitation, never REPRODUCES the object. It creates an ANALOGOUS object.

This analogous object, unlike its "full-scale" counterpart, can be taken in at a glance. Lévi-Strauss uses the phrase "weighed in the palm of one's hand". Through the analogue object, a deeper understanding of the "real" object is arrived at. One of the key functions of art, in the Lévi-Straussian canon, is that it furthers human understanding. The work of art must always fulfil for Lévi-Strauss what he calls a *fonction de connaissance* – a cognitive function.

THE HIDDEN STRUCTURE OF THINGS

The genius of **Jean-Auguste Ingres** (1780–1867), for Lévi-Strauss, is the ability to create the illusion of the objects he represents – such as his famous cashmere shawls – and to go beyond perception to arrive at an understanding of the structure of the object of perception.

Through the work of art, certain fundamental properties (structures) common to the work of art and to the object it represents are brought to light.

The work of art thus provides a road of access to an understanding of the hidden structure of objects.

And these structures, Lévi-Strauss claims, are the very structures the work of art has in common with the structure and functioning of the mind.

Through the work of art, the spectator becomes aware of the functioning of the mind as an object.

MYTHS OF THE AMERICAN INDIANS

Lévi-Strauss's ideas on primitive myth began to take shape early on in the 1950s when he was still teaching at the department of comparative religions at the Ecole Pratique des Hautes Etudes. But it was not until 1964 that he published the first volume of his tetralogy on Amerindian myth, *The Raw and the Cooked*. *From Honey to Ashes* followed in 1967, *The Origin of Table Manners* in 1968 and *The Naked Man* in 1971.

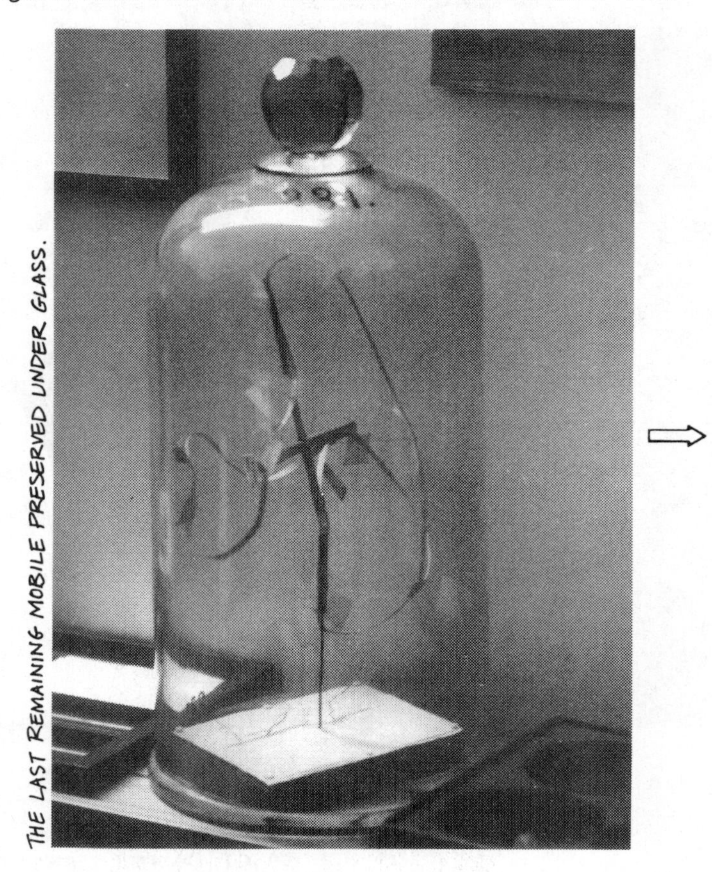

THE LAST REMAINING MOBILE PRESERVED UNDER GLASS.

Lévi-Strauss's passion for Amerindian myth was all-consuming. About this period of his life, he says: "For twenty years, waking up at dawn, I immersed myself in myths . . . I used to live with all these populations, and with their myths as if in a fairy tale." In the laboratory of social anthropology at the Collège de France, Lévi-Strauss made three-dimensional paper models of some of the myths he was studying and hung them from the ceiling like mobiles.

The *Mythologiques*, the name given to the tetralogy as a whole, impress first of all because of their monumental scale. Lévi-Strauss studied a total of 813 complete myths and numerous minor variants in a work over 2,000 pages long that defies categorization. It is at once a collection of mythical stories (that Lévi-Strauss compares to a collage by Max Ernst), an anthropological treatise, an investigation into the functioning of the human mind, a poetic creation (the "myth of Amerindian mythology", says Lévi-Strauss) and a meditation on the nature of the relationship between myth and music.

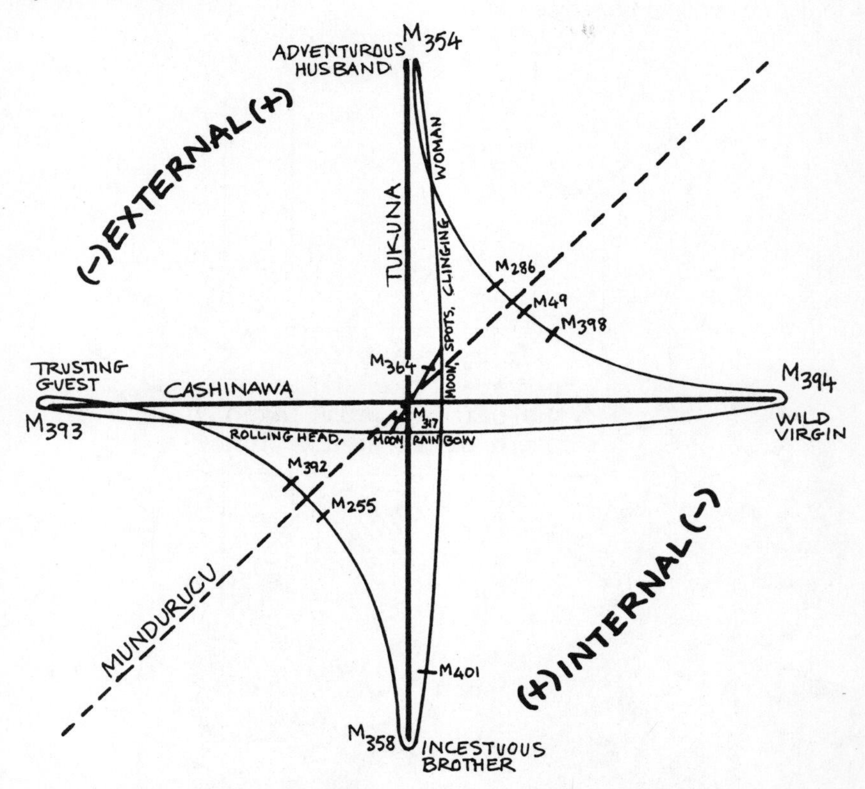

ADVENTUROUS HUSBAND
M354
(–)EXTERNAL(+)
TUKUNA
WOMAN
CLINGING
SPOTS,
MOON,
M286
M49
M398
M364
TRUSTING GUEST
CASHINAWA
M393
M394
WILD VIRGIN
M317
ROLLING HEAD,
MOON
RAINBOW
M392
M255
MUNDURUCU
(+)INTERNAL(–)
M401
M358
INCESTUOUS BROTHER

GROUP STRUCTURE OF TUKUNA, CASHINAWA AND MUNDURUCU MYTHS

How do the *Mythologiques* fit into the rest of Lévi-Strauss's works? They are essentially a continuation of the project he began with *The Elementary Structures of Kinship*. Through myth, Lévi-Strauss aims to arrive at a better understanding of the elementary modes of functioning of the human mind in its capacities for logical thinking. Lévi-Strauss is interested in the intellect.

WHAT IS MYTH?

Myths are a "magnifying glass of the way in which man has always thought".

The study of myths is to Lévi-Strauss what the study of dreams was to Freud: the "royal road" to the unconscious. But the Lévi-Straussian unconscious is empty of any contents; a place where laws of structural patterning are applied to elements (images, memories, emotions, drives) that always come from elsewhere.

In my quest for universal paradigms, myths offer a privileged terrain of investigation.

In his early work, the elementary structures that Lévi-Strauss extracted from the vast mass of kinship systems were meant to reflect the functioning of the mind that had engendered them. However, the possibility always remained that these structures arose out of a different set of determinants. They reflected, for example, certain material constraints of social life that had become objectified in the institutions of kinship exchange.

Not so with myth, says Lévi-Strauss.

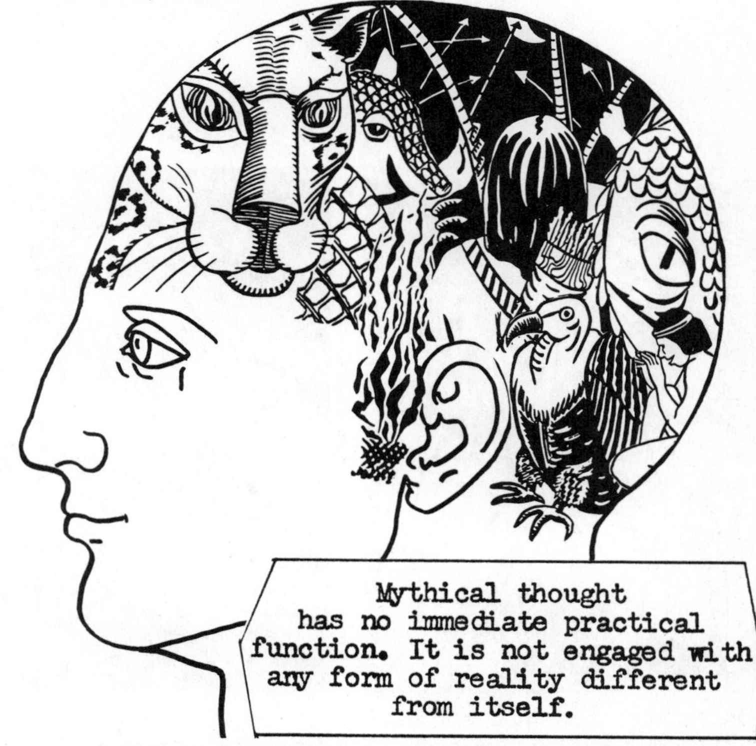
Mythical thought has no immediate practical function. It is not engaged with any form of reality different from itself.

In myth, the mind imitates itself as object, thus reflecting, in as clear a mirror as one may hope to find, the mind's own modes of operating. Lévi-Strauss takes primitive myths to be a manifestation of the free functioning of the mind, observed relatively undisturbed by other extraneous factors. They present an image of the mind in a state of nature.

For anyone who has never come across a primitive myth, the first appeal of the *Mythologiques* will be in the discovery of this unique form of literary creation. The myths – all of them orally transmitted stories, that have no identifiable author and whose origins are lost in time – strike one first of all by their sheer force of invention and unbridled imagination, and this despite their apparent incoherence.

A SAMPLE MYTH

The Shipaia from Brazil have a myth (M178 in *The Raw and the Cooked*) that tells of the origin of the colour of birds. It runs as follows.

Once upon a time, two brothers and a sister lived together in an abandoned hut. One of the brothers fell in love with his sister. He visited her at night without revealing who he was. The other brother found out that his sister was pregnant and told her to mark her secret visitor with genipa dye.

The culprit, thus unmasked, fled to the sky with his sister.

But once there, they argued and the incestuous brother pushed his sister who fell to the earth like a meteorite, landing with a great crash.

There, she transformed into a tapir, while her brother in the sky became the moon.

The moon's human brother ordered the tribe warriors to assemble and shoot arrows at the moon and kill it. Only the armadillo hit his target.

The moon's blood was of many colours and it streamed to earth, splashing the men and women below.

The women wiped themselves with an upward movement, and from that day they are subjected to the influence of the moon. The men wiped themselves with a downward movement.

The birds bathed in the different-coloured pools of blood, and this is how each acquired its unique plumage.

GUIDELINES TO A STUDY OF MYTHS

Contrary to traditional approaches to the study of myths (psychological or symbolic), Lévi-Strauss does not believe them to have a determinate content which it is the analyst's job to recover. Myths are not "reservoirs" of encoded meaning.

Myths are **structures** that realize themselves in and through the listener (in this respect, their meaning is always local). "A myth, like a piece of music, is a score whose silent executors are the audience."

Lévi-Strauss's approach to understanding myth is, at heart, that of an artist, someone concerned with the processes of *creation* of mythical stories and with their internal organization. At the centre of his concerns is the question of how myths come into being. How are they produced?

Understanding what a myth is, is intimately related to understanding a process essentially of *transformation*. Lévi-Strauss's basic hypothesis is that myths come into being by a process of transformation of one myth into another.

Myths do not have any meaning in themselves, but only in relation to each other. In this respect they form a system – one that is analogous to the phonological system which underlies language.

Contrary to what mythographers had done in the past, Lévi-Strauss does not set out to identify the "original" or the "correct" version of a given myth – the Oedipus myth, for example. Rather, he defines a myth as the *sum total of its variants*. In the case of the Oedipus myth, this will also include Freud's interpretation of it, which is no more than its latest transformation (here, into the psycho-sexual code).

To illustrate Lévi-Strauss's method as it is applied in the *Mythologiques* is difficult because wherever one starts, one is always breaking into a chain (or even several chains) of transformations. Equally, wherever one stops will always fall short of arriving somewhere, as it is in the very nature of myths always to be in the process of becoming other myths, none of which contains the final meaning.

The paths of transformation that Lévi-Strauss follows are complicated. It is not simply a question of one myth transforming into another in a unilinear progression. Myths are organized into affiliated groups which form *series* of transformations. But each myth from a series also contains motifs that are transformations of motifs present in myths belonging to other groups or series. The overall picture that emerges is one of multi-dimensional networks of bisecting axes of transformation, an endless criss-crossing of stories.

And as one follows the transformations charted by Lévi-Strauss throughout the *Mythologiques*, one also finds oneself voyaging from the region where one had started off. From a series of myths told by a group of tribes living in central Brazil, Lévi-Strauss traces an uninterrupted chain to the coastal regions of North-Western America, thus linking together the two broad mythological systems of North and South America.

Let us now have a sample of transformation. We begin with Lévi-Strauss's reference myth and point of departure, M1. This is a myth told by the Bororo about the origin of wind and rain-water.

THE BORORO MYTH (M1)

A son guilty of having committed incest with his mother is sent by his father to confront the souls of the dead. He escapes, but his father, still eager to avenge himself, invites him on a bird-nesting trip.

He tricks his son into climbing a steep cliff, where he abandons him for dead. The son survives with the assistance of vultures who, although at first hostile, finally help him to the ground.

The boy returns to his village where he is first recognized by his grandmother who is also his protector. On the night of his arrival, there is a great storm.

All the camp fires in the village are extinguished except for the grandmother's, in whose hut the boy is staying. The following morning, all the members of the village pay a visit to the boy and his grandmother to ask them for hot embers.

Having become aware of his father's presence in the village, the boy sets out to avenge himself for the way he has been treated by him. Using a branch shaped like a deer's antler he charges upon his father, impaling him and then recipitating him into a lake where he is devoured by the spirits of carnivorous fish.

Finally, the boy decides to leave his village, declaring that he would no longer live with his people who had treated him badly. And to punish them he sends them wind and rain.

Lévi-Strauss shows in *The Raw and the Cooked* that the Bororo myth about the bird-nester (M1) belongs to a group of myths told by neighbouring tribes belonging to the Gé linguistic community (M7–M12) which have all got to do with the origin of fire. The Bororo myth is a transformation (an inversion) of the Gé myths (M7–M12). It is a myth about the origin of fire metamorphosed into a myth about the origin of water.

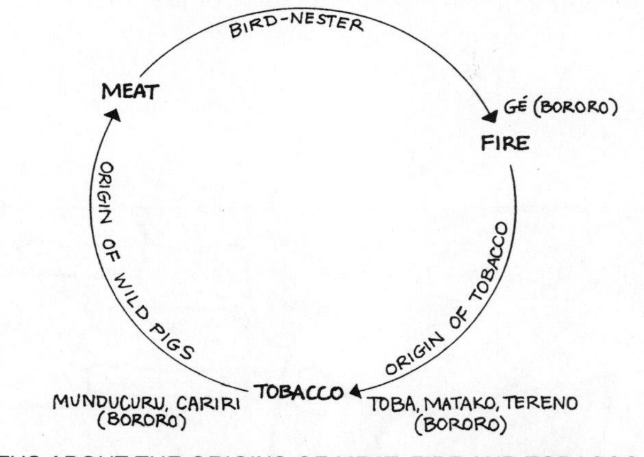
BIRD-NESTER
MEAT
GÉ (BORORO)
FIRE
ORIGIN OF WILD PIGS
ORIGIN OF TOBACCO
TOBACCO
MUNDUCURU, CARIRI
(BORORO)
TOBA, MATAKO, TERENO
(BORORO)

MYTHS ABOUT THE ORIGINS OF MEAT, FIRE AND TOBACCO
FROM *THE RAW AND THE COOKED*

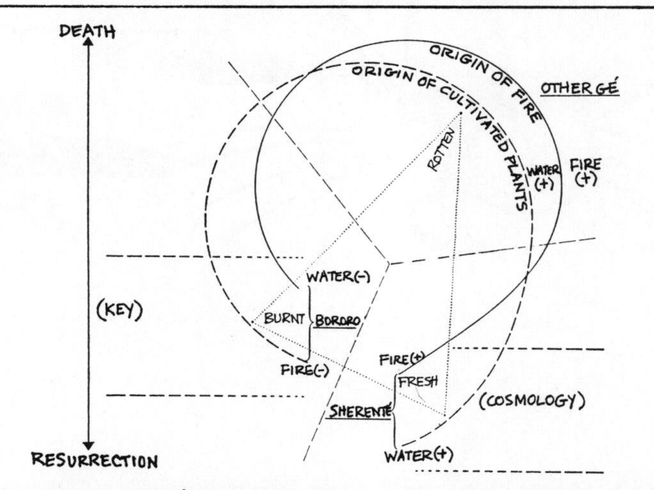
DEATH
ORIGIN OF FIRE
ORIGIN OF CULTIVATED PLANTS
OTHER GÉ
ROTTEN
WATER (+)
FIRE (+)
WATER(-)
(KEY)
BURNT
BORORO
FIRE(-)
FIRE(+)
FRESH
SHERENTÉ
(COSMOLOGY)
WATER(+)
RESURRECTION

INTERRELATION OF GÉ AND BORORO MYTHS ABOUT THE ORIGIN OF FIRE AND CULTIVATED PLANTS FROM *THE RAW AND THE COOKED*

Lévi-Strauss devotes a large part of *The Raw and the Cooked* to demonstrating just how this transformation occurs. It takes a special kind of patience to follow him step by step. A detail will put us on the tracks.

THE POSITION OF THE JAGUAR

The central theme of the Gé series – unrelated, it would seem, to the story told by the Bororo – is that of the alliance between man and jaguar which leads eventually to the acquisition by man of the fire he will use to cook with. Jaguar is the Master of Fire and is described by the myths as having eyes that shine at night like burning embers.

Rain-water in the Bororo myth is conceived as being the opposite of fire because it extinguishes all the fires in the village. It is a kind of "anti-fire", says Lévi-Strauss.

More significantly still, as a result of the storm extinguishing all the village fires except for that of the hero's grandmother, he becomes the sole possessor of fire. Other members of the village must come to him to obtain fire after the storm.

In other words,
he is in the same position
as the jaguar in the Gé myths:
he is the master of fire.

By a process of permutation (a type of inversion), the bird-nester hero has come to take the place of the jaguar.

THE HIDDEN *ARMATURES*

Lévi-Strauss shows that all myths are linked to other myths by relationships of transformation (like the Swaihwé and Dzonokwa masks discussed above). But this is not at the level of their manifest content. Lévi-Strauss identifies a deeper structural level of organization in myths which supports the mythical narrative proper. It is at this level of structural organization that myths may be seen to "communicate with one another".

Lévi-Strauss's method throughout the *Mythologiques* is to dismantle, one by one, the mythical narratives, in order to uncover their hidden *armatures* and determine how these may be related to those underlying other myths. Lévi-Strauss uses the term *armature* in the sense which in French derives from musicology. (In English, an armature is a *key signature*.)

2.Gr.
II.
Ich bin schö - ner!
III.
1.u 2.CHOR (zusam.)
Parsifal.
Vo.
CB. poco cresc.
poco f
poco f
These are the signs written at the beginning of each stave which indicate the tonality or key of a composition. The ARMATURE provides the underlying principle of structural unity.

He breaks up the "diachronic" linearity of the story and shows how it is made up of systems of relationships that may be apprehended "synchronically" as structures. We are reminded of Saussure's idea of diachronic (*parole* or usage) and synchronic (*langue* or language).

BINARY OPPOSITIONS

In the first book of the *Mythologiques*, Lévi-Strauss shows how sensible qualities – such as the raw and the cooked, the fresh and the rotten, the high and the low – are, at the level of deep structure, articulated into systems that encode logical propositions.

The Gé tribe trace the origin of fire to a mythical jaguar. Another series of myths, this time from the Guarani-Tupi, trace the origin of fire to a vulture. Both groups of myths characterize the animals in terms of the types of foods they eat, and it is this which is important about them.

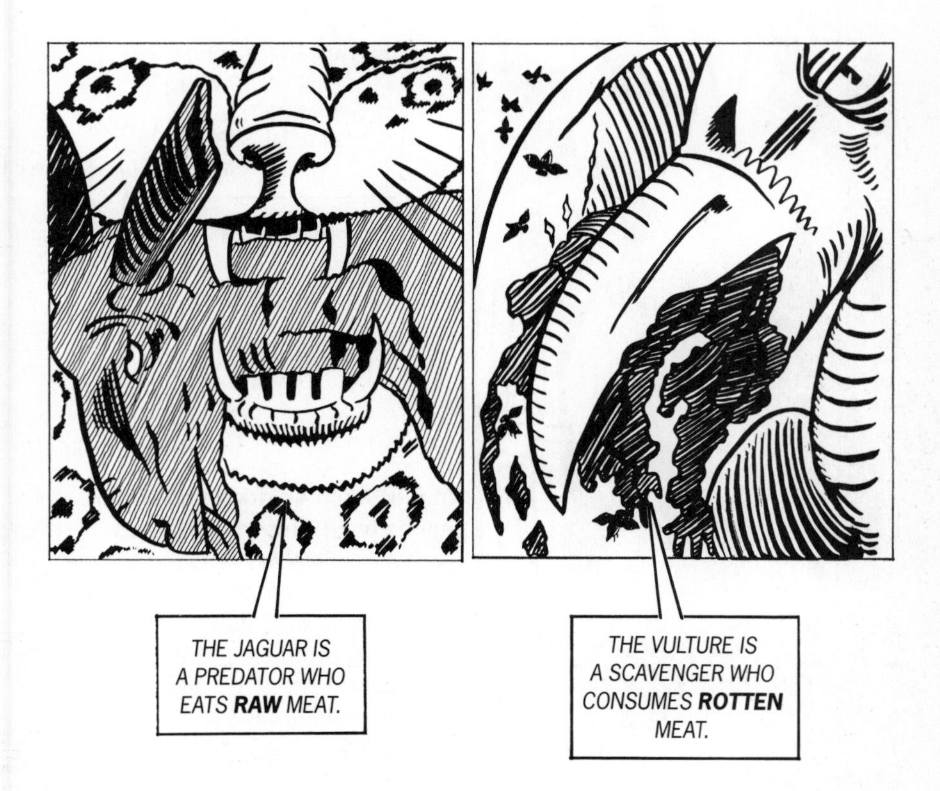
THE JAGUAR IS A PREDATOR WHO EATS **RAW** MEAT.
THE VULTURE IS A SCAVENGER WHO CONSUMES **ROTTEN** MEAT.

The jaguar and the vulture are terms in a system. They are "mythemes" (the "phonemes" of myths) which serve to encode a double opposition, that between the raw and the cooked and that between the fresh and the rotten.

What is the significance of these binary oppositions?

FROM NATURE TO CULTURE

The great theme which all myths have in common is the passage from nature to culture.

A MYTH IS A STORY THAT TAKES PLACE AT A TIME WHEN HUMANS AND ANIMALS WERE NOT YET DISTINCT BEINGS. AND ALL MYTHS, IN THE END, EXPLAIN HOW THIS FUNDAMENTAL, THIS INAUGURAL SEPARATION OCCURRED.

In the South American corpus of myths (with which the first two volumes of the *Mythologiques* are primarily concerned), Lévi-Strauss reveals that it is through cooking – the transformation of the raw into the cooked – that the passage from nature to culture is symbolized. This explains the importance of stories relating to the acquisition by man of the fire he cooks with. Fire occupies a crucial position in mythical thought as a mediating term between, on the one hand, nature and culture, and on the other, the earth and the sky.

The Raw and the Cooked is concerned primarily with the culinary code, but there are many others: astronomical, zoological, social, sexual, etc., and each code has its own generativity. Around the central binary opposition between the raw and the cooked, other elements find their place. One such element is **honey**.

Honey constitutes an essentially ambivalent element in the system. Although it is ready for human consumption (in a sense "cooked"), it has been transformed not by cultural means but by nature itself.

MYTHS AND PARADOXES

In the myths of the North American corpus (in the third and fourth volumes of the *Mythologiques*), the symbols change. What marks the passage from nature to culture is no longer the symbolic mediation of cooking, but the invention of costumes, ornaments and the institution of commercial exchanges. Thus, where South American myths oppose the raw to the cooked, North American myths oppose the naked to the clothed.

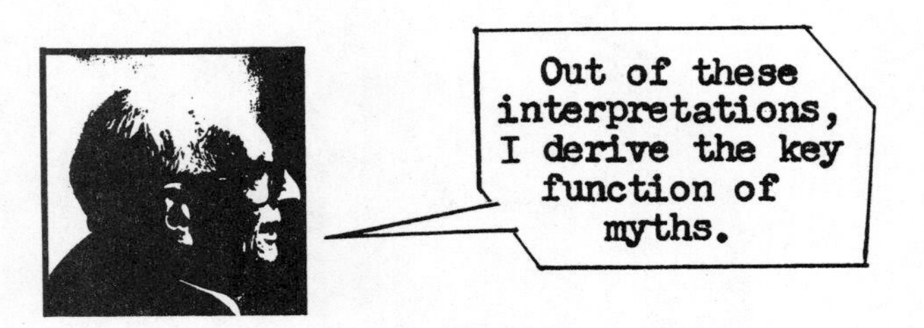
Out of these interpretations, I derive the key function of myths.

In a nutshell, his conception is that myths are tools for processing logical problems. They are invented to mediate fundamental paradoxes or contradictions within a culture that cannot be solved.

These paradoxes are of numerous kinds: metaphysical, moral, social, legal, political, religious, etc. And they provide the impetus which sets mythical thought in motion. Myths do not aim to resolve the paradoxes around which they develop, in the way philosophy does. The "solution" they provide is other. Their principle virtue is to transpose these paradoxes into the terms of other, similar, paradoxes. Thus, myths develop in a kind of spiral, by establishing a series of analogies between formally similar problems.

to complete happiness
seeks happiness with
successful, romantic
for love
caring & aware
nature & beauty
for loving, sharing
to share talking, walking
TO THE QUESTION: WHO SHOULD I MARRY?, AMERINDIAN MYTH ANSWERS . . .
SOMEONE WHO IS NEITHER FURTHER NOR CLOSER THAN, IN THE ALTERNATION OF NIGHT AND DAY, THE MOON IS TO THE SUN.

DO MYTHS HAVE MEANING?

For Lévi-Strauss, a myth is not a reservoir of archetypes or universal symbols, as **C.G. Jung** (1875–1961) believed myths to be. The images it assembles are chosen first of all for their "symbolic efficacy", their capacity to express metaphorically (encode) a particular set of problems. What the Argentinian writer **Jorge Luis Borges** (1899–1986) said about that grandfather of mythical beings, the dragon, is true of the Lévi-Straussian view of myths.

We are ignorant of the meaning of the dragon in the same way that we are ignorant of the meaning of the universe, but there is something in the dragon's image that fits man's imagination, and this accounts for the dragon's appearance in different places and periods.
(*The Book of Imaginary Beings*)

Meaning is not *in* myths – rather myths, and the images they invent, are structures *through which* to make sense of the rest of the world.

"A myth offers a grid that is definable only by its rules of construction. This grid enables one to decipher the meaning, not of the myth itself, but of all the rest: images of the world, of society, of history, which lie at the fringe of consciousness, along with all the questions we ask about them." [CL-S]

A myth is a
"matrix of intelligibility".

THE OEDIPUS MYTH

Lévi-Strauss also turned his attention to literary texts in Western culture. One example is the Greek myth of Oedipus which emerged from ancient local legends and folklore, best known to us in its dramatized version by **Sophocles** (c. 496–406 B.C.).

Oedipus may originally have been related to an underground or snake god. His name means "swollen-foot" and can be interpreted as an anthropomorphic figuration of a dragon's tail. Lévi-Strauss has compared the inability to "walk straight" (Oedipus = swollen foot) to being born from the earth, a Greek chthonic belief. Central to the myth is a concern with man's origins.

The story, as most commonly told, is this. Oedipus is the son of King Laius (of the Theban dynasty founded by the dragon-slayer Cadmus) and Queen Jocasta.

Laius learns from an oracle that his son will one day murder him and marry Jocasta. Laius commands that the baby be left to die on Mount Cithaeron with his feet pierced (swollen-foot).

But Oedipus is saved by a shepherd and he grows to manhood unaware who his real parents are.

One day, on his journeys, Oedipus comes to a crossroads. He enters into conflict with an arrogant stranger and kills him. This man is none other than his own father, Laius. Oedipus has unknowingly committed the great crime of parricide.

He proceeds to Thebes which is oppressed by a devouring monster, the Sphinx. He solves the Sphinx's riddle and thus forces her to kill herself (like his ancestor Cadmus, Oedipus too is a dragon-slayer).

In reward, Oedipus is offered the throne of Thebes and the hand of Laius's widow, Jocasta, his mother.

Thebes is consequently ravaged by a dreadful plague. For it to end, the Delphic oracle commands that the slayer of Laius be found.

Oedipus takes on the task and discovers he is himself the killer he is looking for. When his identity is revealed, Jocasta hangs herself and Oedipus blinds himself with her brooch.

THE INTERPRETATION

Lévi-Strauss focuses on the episode of the Sphinx at the heart of the Oedipus legend. Solving the Sphinx's riddle leads Oedipus to incest with his mother – which is also ironically his reward, to become King of Thebes and marry the Queen.

In Lévi-Strauss's unravelling of this mytho-poetic logic, the riddle (*énigme*) is defined as a question to which there is no answer. Oedipus therefore unites a question and an answer that should have been kept apart. This exemplifies what may be described as an "excess of communication"; just as the incestuous marriage is an "excess of communication" of a different kind that similarly unites two "terms" best kept apart.

THE PERCIVAL LEGEND

The story of Percival centres on the quest for the miraculous Holy Grail – the cup from which it was believed Christ drank at the Last Supper. The earliest known literary version of the Grail legend is by **Chrestien de Troyes** (1160–90), a poet at the court of Marie de Champagne and Philip of Flanders and the author of some Arthurian romances. He left the Percival story unfinished at his death. **Wolfram von Eschenbach** (c. 1195–1225) provided the most famous elaboration of the story and **Richard Wagner** (1813–83) based his opera *Parsifal* on it. Lévi-Strauss has a great passion for Wagner.

Percival is often presented as a forest-dweller, a virgin, ignorant of courtly life.

After many awkward mistakes, Percival finally achieves knighthood at King Arthur's Round Table.

In the central episode of the story, Percival is invited to the castle of the Grail by the Fisher-King, mysteriously immobilized by an injury to his legs. Percival dines on a sumptuous meal. There appear before him, first a young man holding a bleeding spear, then two young girls, one holding a jewel-encrusted cup (the Grail) and the other a silver tray with food.

Despite his curiosity, Percival does not dare ask about the spear or who is being served in this way. His decision to remain silent is a terrible mistake. Had he asked the question that was in fact expected of him, the Fisher-King would have been cured and the spell on the land of the Grail, causing its infertility, would have been lifted.

THE INTERPRETATION

Lévi-Strauss compares this episode of Percival's failure to ask with the "excess of communication" that brings Oedipus to his doom. What we find in Percival's case of dysfunctional speech is "the answer to which there is no question", an exact inversion of the riddle that Oedipus confronts.

Oedipus is the clever hero whose answer exceeds "communication" to the point of incest. Percival is the virginal hero who does not know how to ask a question.

Chastity, virginity and impotence are equated with the linguistic figure of an answer to which a question is not provided; incest to the figure of the question which, best left unanswered, is abusively answered.

The world of Oedipus is one of accelerated communication. This is also symbolized by the Theban plague which accelerates or explodes the natural cycles. Excessive communication and incest are associated with rotting and rankness (plague). Conversely, in Percival's world, communication is interrupted. There is a halting of nature's cycles which leads to the infertility of the land, eternal winter and a frozen, immobile world.

In these two myths, Lévi-Strauss has found *transformations* at work. Within what he calls "universal mythology", these stories of Oedipus and Percival constitute two fundamental narrative types whose underlying *armatures* are the inverse of one another.

MYTH AND MUSIC

Lévi-Strauss's theories about myths provide the elements of a complex and original narratological theory or *poetics*. One of the most distinctive features of this poetics is the close affinity that exists in Lévi-Strauss's thought between myth and music.

At the beginning of *The Raw and the Cooked*, he claims that Richard Wagner is the founding father of the structural analysis of myths. Wagner's music reveals hidden structures in the myths that it accompanies.

C
più p
The musical score is a kind of structural interpretation of the libretto.
marcato
Bass: D
E♮
pp
A♭
E♭

One of the key parallels between myth and music is this. A musical score is perceived at once as something unfolding "horizontally" in a linear manner, stave by stave, and as a totality (reconstructed in the mind of the listener during audition) made up also of other "vertical" relationships.

The ability to appreciate a musical formula, such as *theme* and *variation*, demands that for each variation the listener keep in mind the theme which was first heard. Each variation is *superimposed* on earlier variations. This is exactly what Lévi-Strauss does with myths – or what he calls "mythemes" – when he reveals them to be transformations (variations) of other "mythemes".

Lévi-Strauss says about myth . . .

We have to read not only from left to right, but at the same time vertically, from top to bottom, that is, with an ear for "harmonic" as well as "melodic" correspondences.
Hob.
Althob.
Cl.
Hör.
poco
Fag.
Tromp. (F)
cresc.
(Bog.)
(Bog.)

Lévi-Strauss gave the different sections of *The Raw and the Cooked* titles borrowed from music. This is in part because he found, when studying the plots of Amerindian myths, that many of them were constructed in a similar way to musical forms such as fugues, sonatas, rondos, toccatas, etc.

Lévi-Strauss also developed an historical hypothesis about the relationship of myth and music in Western culture.

During the Renaissance and the 17th century, mythical thought passed into the background of Western thought. But it was also at this time that the great musical styles of Western culture – those which became characteristic of the 17th, 18th and 19th centuries, embodied in such figures as Frescobaldi, Bach, Mozart, Beethoven and Wagner – began to emerge.

For Lévi-Strauss, this is no coincidence.

It is exactly as if music had completely changed its traditional shape in order to take over the function – the intellectual as well as the emotive function – which mythical thought was giving up more or less at the same period.

STRUCTURALISM AND THE BODY

Lévi-Strauss has sometimes been accused of being an idealist, of reducing culture to a play of the mind. This is not the case. Lévi-Strauss is a materialist. Ultimately, he traces the logical processes of transformation (permutations, substitutions, inversions, symmetries, etc.) that affect myths (and other aspects of culture) to the way in which our sense organs process the data of perception – i.e., to the *functioning of the body*.

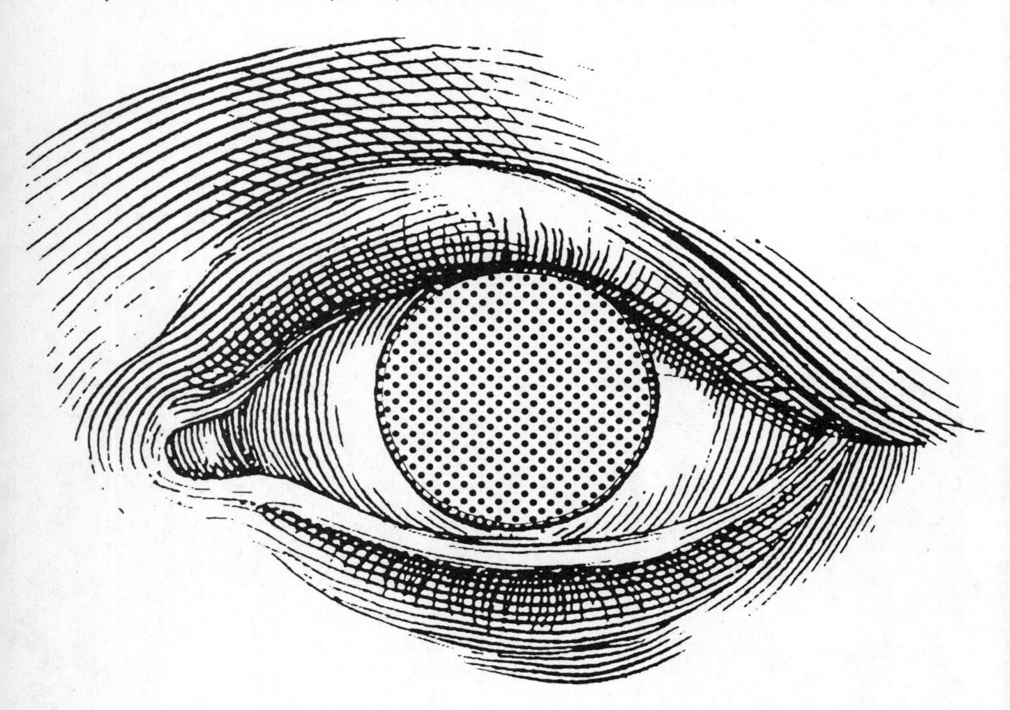

Research into the mechanisms of sight shows that the retina, before relaying information to the brain, already encodes it according to structural rules of patterning. The visual cortex is programmed to discriminate between upward and downward movement, between relatively dark and relatively luminous objects. And it also produces its own structural variations: the yellow glare of a light bulb, when switched off, is replaced by a green circle.

Structural analysis emerges
in the mind only because its model
already exists in the body.

“To speak of rules and to speak of meaning is to speak of the same thing; and if we look at all the intellectual undertakings of mankind, as far as they have been recorded all over the world, the common denominator is always to introduce some kind of order. If this represents a basic need for order in the human mind and since, after all, the human mind is only part of the universe, the need probably exists because there is some order in the universe and the universe is not a chaos.” [CL-S]

Lévi-Strauss, like most neuro-biologists today, rejects the mind/body dualism (inherited from Descartes) that has dominated so much of Western thought. He sees mind and body as functioning together as a single “eco-system”.

In response to the charges of "intellectualism" raised against him, Lévi-Strauss shows how structuralism reunites the sensible and the intelligible. In its final stages, structural analysis restores the full plenitude of that unity.

Lévi-Strauss sees intimate parallels between the ways in which the genetic code determines – through its own form of combinatorial logic – the many forms of life and the structural operations of the brain whose patterns he detects in the products of human culture.

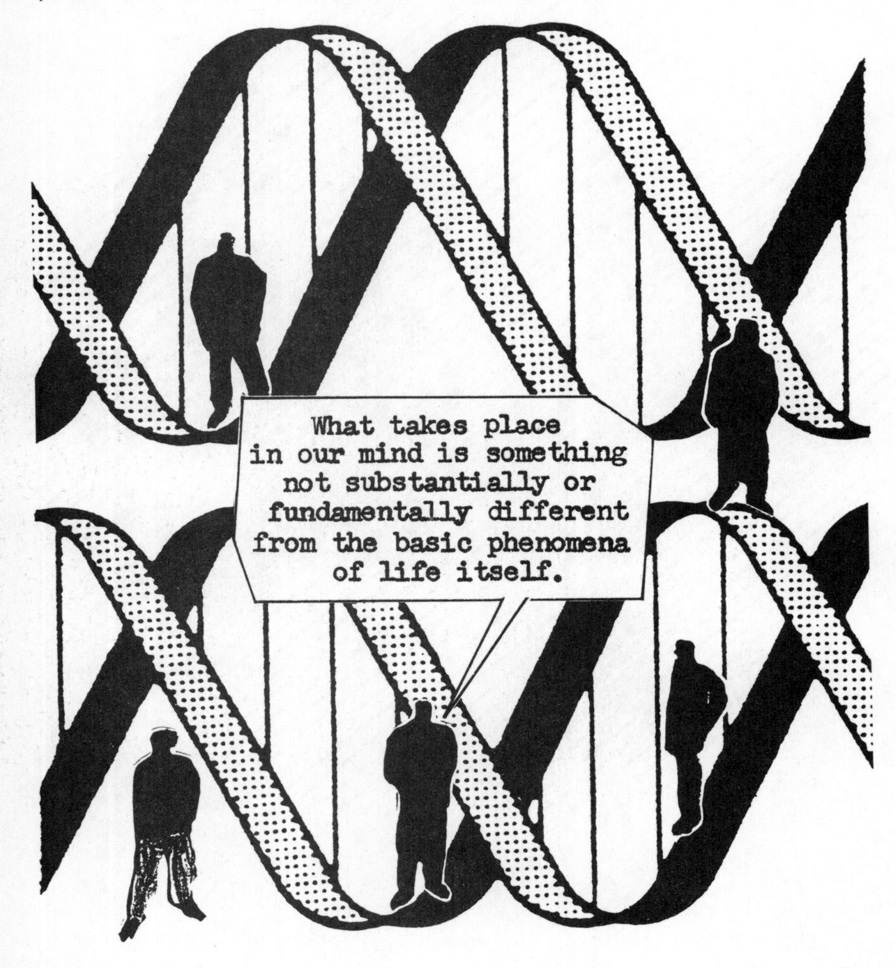
What takes place in our mind is something not substantially or fundamentally different from the basic phenomena of life itself.

Lévi-Strauss's structuralism has stressed the ways in which man is made what he is by structures that lie beyond his control. About myths, he says that they "think themselves in man, unbeknown to him".

As one of the founding fathers of the structuralist movement, his methods and ideas came to have an impact, direct or indirect, on many of his most prominent contemporaries: Jacques Lacan, Roland Barthes, Louis Althusser, Michel Foucault.

DO YOU RECOGNIZE YOURSELF IN THE USE THAT LACAN HAS MADE OF YOUR IDEAS?
No, not at all, but we were friends.

Lévi-Strauss denies that he shares a common system of thought with these other thinkers who have at one time or another been labelled as structuralist.

In the field of anthropology Lévi-Strauss rapidly became, even for those opposed to his ideas, an obligatory point of reference. His influence on literary criticism, philosophy and many other fields has been equally great and controversial. Jacques Derrida's essay "Structure, Sign, and Play in the Discourse of the Human Sciences" (conference paper, 1966; reprinted in *L'écriture et la différence*, 1967) is a confrontation with Lévi-Strauss. It is one of the founding texts of postmodern thought which marks the point where the break with structuralism occurred.

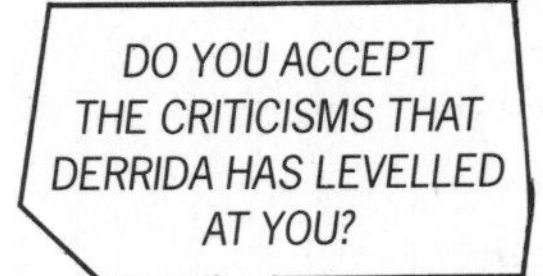
DO YOU ACCEPT THE CRITICISMS THAT DERRIDA HAS LEVELLED AT YOU?
I must confess that I haven't read him closely. He and I do not at all have the same way of writing. I find him difficult to follow.

Contrary to Derrida, whose purpose is to "deconstruct" the edifices of the past (metaphysics, nature, language), Lévi-Strauss is a builder like the mytho-poetic *bricoleur* of his own invention.

... I don't have the feeling that I write my books. I have the feeling that my books get written through me and that once they have got across me I feel empty and nothing is left... I never had, and still do not have, the perception of feeling my personal identity. I appear to myself as the place where something is going on, but there is no "I", no "me". Each of us is a kind of crossroads where things happen. The crossroads is purely passive; something happens there. A different thing, equally valid, happens elsewhere. There is no choice, it is just a matter of chance.

from a radio interview, Canadian Broadcasting Company, 1977

FURTHER READING

Books by Lévi-Strauss

The Savage Mind, London: Weidenfeld & Nicolson, 1966; Chicago: University of Chicago Press, 1966. One of his most complex and influential works.
Tristes Tropiques, London: Jonathan Cape, 1973; *A World on the Wane* (abridged), New York: Criterion Books, 1961. An autobiographical account of his early field trips to central Brazil.
Mythologiques (*Introduction to a Science of Mythology*), 4 vols – *The Raw and the Cooked, From Honey to Ashes, The Origin of Table Manners, The Naked Man*, London: Jonathan Cape, 1970–81; New York: Harper & Row, 1969–82.
The Way of the Masks, London: Jonathan Cape, 1983; Seattle: University of Washington Press, 1982.

Collected essays

Structural Anthropology, London: Allen Lane, 1968; New York: Penguin Books, 1994.
Structural Anthropology (volume 2), London: Allen Lane, 1977; New York: Peregrine Books, 1976.
The View From Afar, Oxford: Blackwell, 1985; New York: Basic Books, 1984.

Conversations and interviews – a good place to start tackling Lévi-Strauss's thought

Conversations with George Charbonnier, London: Jonathan Cape, 1969.
Conversations with Claude Lévi-Strauss, ed. Didier Eribon, Chicago: University of Chicago Press, 1991.
Myth and Meaning, New York: Schocken Books, 1995. Talks broadcast by the Canadian Broadcasting Company, 1977.

Useful introductions to Lévi-Strauss's thought

Claude Lévi-Strauss: The Anthropologist as Hero, ed. E.N. & T. Hayes, Cambridge, Mass.: The M.I.T. Press, 1970. Includes articles by Edmund Leach, George Steiner and Susan Sontag.
Claude Lévi-Strauss, Edmund Leach, London: Fontana 1996; Chicago: University of Chicago Press, 1989.
Claude Lévi-Strauss: an Introduction, Octavio Paz, Ithaca: Cornell University Press, 1970. A poet's viewpoint.

Author's Acknowledgements

I would like to express my gratitude to Claude Lévi-Strauss for having read the manuscript of this book, and for his invaluable comments. I would also like to thank Claude Imbert and Philippe Hamon, whose insightful remarks about Lévi-Strauss have been of great help. However, the interpretation of Lévi-Strauss's ideas, together with any errors or misjudgements, remain entirely my responsibility.

I would like to dedicate this book to my parents.

Artist's Acknowledgements

Judy Groves would like to express her warm appreciation to Claude Lévi-Strauss for allowing her to photograph him for this book. She would also like to thank Madeline Fenton, David King, Claudine Meissner, Howard Peters, Mark Peters, Nick Robin and Oscar Zarate for their invaluable help.

Boris Wiseman is a Lecturer in French at the University of Durham. He studied French and Anthropology at King's College London and the London School of Economics, and has written his PhD on Lévi-Strauss's aesthetic thought.

Judy Groves is an artist, illustrator and designer. She has also illustrated *Philosophy*, *Wittgenstein*, *Lacan*, *Plato*, *Christianity* and *Chomsky* in the *Introducing* series.

Typesetting by **Wayzgoose**

Index